CREATING
THE
"I"
IN
TEAM

CREATING
THE
"I"
IN
TEAM

**Building High Performing Teams
with Intelligence, Initiative, and Integrity**

by
Jeffrey S. McCreary
Senior Vice-President, Texas Instruments
Manager, Worldwide Sales & Marketing (retired)

With a Foreword
by
Ken Hitchcock
Stanley Cup Champion,
National Hockey League (NHL) Head Coach

SUNSTONE
PRESS
SANTA FE

Book design by Vicki Ahl

Sunstone books may be purchased for educational, business, or sales promotional use. For information please write: Special Markets Department, Sunstone Press, P.O. Box 2321, Santa Fe, New Mexico 87504-2321.

Library of Congress Cataloging-in-Publication Data

McCreary, Jeffrey S., 1956-
    Creating the "I" in team : building high performing teams with intelligence, initiative, and integrity / by Jeffrey S. McCreary ; with a foreword by Ken Hitchcock.
        p. cm.
    ISBN 0-86534-538-4 (hardcover : alk. paper)
    1. Teams in the workplace--Management. 1. Title.

HD66.M383 2007
658.4'022--dc22

                                                2006038143

Published in

WWW.SUNSTONEPRESS.COM
SUNSTONE PRESS / POST OFFICE BOX 2321 / SANTA FE, NM 87504-2321 /USA
(505) 988-4418 / ORDERS ONLY (800) 243-5644 / FAX (505) 988-1025

CONTENTS

FOREWORD

by
Ken Hitchcock
Stanley Cup Champion,
National Hockey League (NHL) Head Coach

The world of sports is the ultimate competitive environment. It is the one business that keeps score each and every day. When you compete, someone wins and someone loses. That is probably why there is so much fascination with sports from business leaders. Although their time frames might be longer, business leaders feel the same competitive pressures as coaches, general managers and owners. Plus, they appreciate the need to operate with teams. It is actually those teams that will be the key to their success. I believe strongly that you must build the team before you can rightfully expect to win. To win, and win consistently you will have to become a builder of great teams. Within each team, you will have to build an atmosphere of companionship and sacrifice. You will have to convince people that there is great value in their individual role whatever it may be. You will have to get each individual committed to being a small part of something bigger. When you look to put a winning program together, it is always the sum of the parts that equals success. That is why, whether your team is built in the world of business or the world of sports, you might use a quote like: "There is no I in team!"

I love the game of hockey. It is a big part of my life. But, I actually enjoy building and molding the team as much as the competition itself. Finding and developing the pieces required for success is rewarding and it is what I enjoy the most. I love watching a team raise their level of commitment and sacrifice as they come together.

I have certainly seen many different styles of leadership work. But no matter how they do it, the leader's number one job is to provide enthusiasm and hope on a daily basis. The leader must create the atmosphere for success. The leader must build connections throughout the organization to move it towards their goals. The most successful leaders bring conviction, compassion, enthusiasm, and commitment to their role. They reach down, not yell down into their organizations. And, they understand the importance of showing appreciation for a job well done. Real leaders constantly acknowledge success in the workplace. This is especially important in the business world where there is not the constant attention of media to provide feedback that supports the team.

The leadership of the organization will face many demands. At the forefront is the fact that the job is twenty-four hours per day, seven days a week. How leaders handle themselves in public and how they handle themselves in private will be evaluated and will matter. They are the image of the organization. Although they share in the success, leaders don't have the luxury of enjoying any victory too long. They must be the first to get the team moving ahead to the next challenge.

To meet that next challenge you will have to get better along the way. I look for self-improvement on a daily basis. I know that long term success can not be achieved without real commitment to continuous improvement. Great leaders, in each and every field, are never satisfied. They are always working to get better. When you get satisfied you stagnate and then quickly start going backwards. That is why I am always searching for something that will improve my performance and give me an edge. I have always been intrigued by the success of others. Whether that success comes in sports, in business, in academia, in music, or wherever—I have found important ideas to learn from. I think the biggest form of flattery anyone can receive is to have their ideas and work copied. I am constantly evaluating the work of others in an effort to improve my own performance. So whether it is my idea being copied or me copying someone else's ideas I am aware of the compliment implied by that act.

I have engaged with many business executives over the years, who were eager to learn from sports. Yet, there is no question that sports has a lot to learn from the business world as well. I routinely search to learn how business leaders organize their resources, how they stay focused on the right targets, and how they keep a large organization committed to reaching their goals. The best of those business leaders show a keen ability to make it more than just a job for their people.

This book's author, Jeff McCreary, is certainly one of those proven business leaders I have learned from. Jeff brings energy, passion, and focus to all the organizations I have seen him engage with. I have watched Jeff work with different groups within his global organization and even with his customers. He has a great ability to keep people on task and committed to do the job right…all the way to the end.

That is why I am confident that anyone interested in improving their performance as a leader and in building better teams can learn from this book.

At the end of the day, you must remember that your success will come from your people. We are all focused on winning. Winning will certainly bring you security. Yet a real leader will recognize that they are in the people business. The business of winning starts with being successful in the people business. The most powerful attribute you can develop in the people business is to become a builder of great teams.

PREFACE

"There's no I in team!"

Coaches shout it in locker rooms around the word. And supervisors in the business world also repeat it like well-schooled parrots as they challenge their organizations.

"There's no I in team!" It is certainly one of the most exalted of all sports clichés—more personal than "Put up or shut up," easier to prove than "We need to give 110%," more credible than "We're taking it one game at a time."

"There's no I in team!" Apparently a lot of folks really believe it.

What a glorious ode to the sanctity of the team. What a selfless expression of the importance of working for the greater good. What a triumphant reminder of the importance of sacrifice.

What a dangerously misleading and inaccurate witticism.

Sure, the letter "I" doesn't appear in the word "team." Nor does it appear in the word "person," nor in "watermelon." So what?

Clichés don't make teams run smoothly and effectively—people do. The truth is that "I" is in every team, and to deny that is to deny the very foundation on which a team is built. It obviously starts with the fact that teams are made up of individuals. Success demands that you reach every individual on the team. However, this book is about much more than that element. This is about creating superior team performance by focusing on the "I" of Intelligence, Initiative, and Integrity.

There is almost no challenge you will face in life that cannot be met more effectively through the power of a team. You will accomplish more, get it done more quickly, and have more fun doing it with a strong team. If you're ready to change the world and leave a lasting mark on your chosen field, a high-performing team is precisely what you will need. Building great teams in business and in sports is a daunting task. It is talked about endlessly, yet surprisingly few managers consistently demonstrate the capability to pull it off.

For the individual committed to building better teams, there is certainly no shortage of material to draw upon. You can attend seminars, employ the most skilled consultants, hire personal coaches, and read a library full of books. This plethora of material suggests we all have a lot of room for improvement. Obviously, you are aware of these challenges and searching for something that might just give you that competitive edge. Building better teams is your responsibility. This book will guide you, but it will be your energy, commitment, and audacity that make it happen.

I expect to deliver three specific outcomes in this book:

1. **Provide simple but effective guidelines for building better teams.**

2. **Reinforce the need to cultivate Intelligence, Initiative, and Integrity.**
3. **Inspire you to excel in your role as a leader.**

So let this book inspire and inform you and help you learn how to change your world for the better because, above all, that's what powerful teams do.

ACKNOWLEDGEMENTS

It seems essential that a book on team building should start with an acknowledgement that it took a team to bring this particular book to fruition. My deep appreciation and thanks go first and most importantly to my wife, Syndii. She has been and continues to be the most powerful force in my life. There is no question that I became a better leader through her positive, patient, and gracious guidance. My two sons (Connor and Max) have been a great influence on my perspectives as well. They continue to teach me about what is really important in life. Together, with my wife, they have provided a stable foundation and a dose of maturity that added to my success in the workplace and brought me unmatched joy.

I have tried to learn something from each and every book I have ever read. There is no question that a limitless number of authors have influenced my perspectives and my work. Books like Allan Cox's *Straight Talk for Monday Morning*, Dorothy Leeds' *Smart Questions*, Warren Bennis's *Leaders*, Harvey Mackay's *Swim with the*

Sharks, John Naisbitt's *Megatrends*, Tom Peters' *In Search of Excellence* and *A Passion for Excellence* and everything Peter Druker wrote had enormous influence over me early in my mid-level management days. In the past decade I have been moved by the work of Jim Collins (*Good to Great*), M Buckingham and C Coffman (*First Break All the Rules*), J Katzenbach and D Smith (*The Wisdom of Teams*), Chris Meyer (*Fast Cycle Time*), Peter Senge (*The Fifth Discipline*), Clayton Christensen (*The Innovator's Dilemma*), Ken Blanchard and Spencer Johnson (*The One Minute Manager* and *Who Moved my Cheese*), and a host of others. I am sure many of their perspectives show up in my work. I would only ask anyone who reads my views and believes they are their own to understand that imitation truly is the most sincere form of flattery. When it comes to team building, I have been trying to imitate the success of others for many years.

In the book I also mention a number of key people who had great influence on my beliefs and the processes I use. A few deserve special mention here as well. Rich Templeton (Texas Instruments CEO) is quite simply the most impressive executive I have ever been around. Kevin McGarity (Texas Instruments Sr. Vice President—retired) was my boss before I took over the worldwide sales and marketing team. He operated with unmatched integrity and loyalty. He was fearless in facing complex issues. Gene McFarland (Texas Instruments Vice President—retired) was the first TI officer that I reported directly to. He was a disciplined leader who operated with tremendous poise. The late Glenn Culhane (Texas Instruments Vice President) was the most colorful manager I ever worked for. He was insightful, relentless and passionate. Sam Hulbert (Rose-Hulman Institute of Technology, President—retired) brought extraordinary vision, passion and commitment to his twenty-eight years at Rose. I am honored to have graduated when Sam was President and to have joined the Board of

Trustees while he was still there. Ron Reeves (Rose-Hulman Institute of Technology, Vice President for Development and External Affairs— retired) was the most loyal, understanding, and high integrity person I have every engaged with. Hal Brown and Bob Bright (Rose-Hulman Board of Trustees) taught me about stewardship, responsibility, and commitment from my earliest days of interaction with them. Those folks, and a host of others deserve my thanks.

It is also important that I thank the many people who worked within my organizations and taught me so much. I have never been confused regarding how challenging it can be to work for me. I am demanding, passionate, outspoken, and seldom easily satisfied. My greatest strengths come coupled with some weaknesses as well. However, my teams always found a way to press past my shortfalls and to embrace my commitment to our mutual success. I thank each and every person who has been a part of one of my teams over the years. John Szczsponik (Texas Instruments Senior Vice President) and Brian Bonner (Texas Instruments Vice President) probably tolerated me the longest without any serious damage to their careers. I likely learned more from them than they did from me. Kerri-Ann Walker (currently a Senior Vice President at Bank of America) supported my organization as a leadership consultant for a number of critical years. She was a positive force for our organizations, its leaders, and for me personally. At the risk of leaving someone important out, others that I learned from within my organization include Zoe Chapman, Karen Golshan, Mike Walker, Craig Rhodine, Larry Tan, Beth Bull, Leo McGahan, Paul Carson, Jean Francios Fau (who dual reported to the CEO), Alain Mutricy, Marcia Page, Doug Rasor, Mike O'Brien and a host of others. Last but not least among this group was my administrative assistant at TI for over a dozen years, Sally Lott. Again, I thank them all.

Finally, some special thanks to those who were especially helpful as I was putting the book together. Thank-you to:

Paco Garza, of Garza Communications, for creating an impressive proposal when I was shopping the book idea to publishers.

Journalist Melissa Geschwind who helped improve my early "Introduction" during the proposal stage and who would have ghost written for me and Ken Hitchcock had we decided to go down that route.

Stan Slap for showing me what a first rate book proposal really looked like and for motivating me to improve my efforts.

Neal Lyon, Santa Fe real estate agent extraordinaire, for hooking me up with Jim Smith at Sunstone Press.

Steve Bakota, Neal Brenner, Nancy Buckles, Ivan DeFur, and Greg Kitchen for their feedback on my drafts.

Especially Bob Fyfe, Gary Gilbert and Kerri-Ann Walker for their detailed reviews and extensive suggestions.

I extol the greatness of National Hockey League coach Ken Hitchcock many times in the book. However, he deserves special thanks here as well for allowing me to use his perspectives and some of his material, for his commitment to the success of my organizations, and for his friendship.

To Jim Smith at Sunstone Press, a special thank you for believing in the project and for your patient guidance and support. You and Carl Condit are gems.

THE ROLE OF LEADERSHIP

My target audience for this book has always been leaders. In particular, I have tried to expose perspectives and tools for leaders (managers, supervisors, etc.) who are relatively new to the role and are searching for ways to improve their performance. As such, it seems appropriate to first spend some time on the role of leaders.

What is a leader? There is certainly no shortage of definitions and perspectives on the topic. There are books, tapes, videos, and more on the topic. You can go to seminars; you can even hire a personal coach to help you with the subject. Interestingly, the definitions tend to change over time and are variable on a regional basis. Descriptions of leadership are also influenced by current culture, world events, and academic trends. At one time in history, leadership was thrust upon individuals as a birthright. Today, we embrace a more democratic process.

Here are a few definitions.

Warren Bennis is known the world over for his study and

assessment of leadership. In his book, *Leaders* (with Burt Nanus), he describes leadership as, "The wise use of power." He further clarifies power as, "The capacity to translate intention into reality and to sustain it." What I believe Bennis has described is people who get things done.

I distinctly remember hearing Rich Templeton (COO of Texas Instruments at the time) answer a question about leadership. As a company, we were working hard to establish and disseminate what we felt was a very important set of leadership doctrines. In a public forum, someone asked Rich if he would define leadership from his perspective. Rich quickly expressed that he felt there were many different styles of effective leadership, but at the end of the day, "Leaders must create and maintain followers." I have read a lot of books on this topic, and I have heard a lot of smart and talented folks speak about leadership. For me, Rich's view is as simple and yet as powerful as it gets. It is people power that provides the capacity to make things happen. The leaders get the group moving and keep it moving.

Former National Basketball Association (NBA) and current Louisville basketball coach (and author), Rick Pitino, said, "Teams that have strong leadership have a decided advantage. If you look at the great NBA teams of the past fifteen years, one of the common threads is they all had great veteran leaders with the group: Larry Bird (Celtics), Magic Johnson (Lakers), Isaiah Thomas (Pistons), Michael Jordan (Bulls). Each had his own style, but they all demanded excellence from the people around them."

There is no shortage of respected and proven coaches who share this belief. The impact of leadership is unquestioned. A winning team will be intelligent. An intelligent team will know their roles. The role of leader will be valued and nurtured.

I feel that great leaders are those who enable the success of others. This, for me, is almost a definition of leadership, coaching, and management. Certainly, the more senior your position in an organization the more important your role in developing leaders will be. As you progress, your most essential task may well become the identification, development, and empowerment of other leaders.

One of the most important pieces of knowledge that you and your other leaders should embrace is that the vast majority of people really want to be successful, both individually and as an organization/team.

Leadership carries great responsibilities. There are lots of expectations that come with being in leadership positions. There are expectations from above and from below. The more you can address these expectations with your leaders, the more effective they will be and the more intelligent your team will be.

The best leaders are able to articulate a vision. They speak convincingly about what the team is trying to accomplish and why it is worth working toward that goal. Well expressed, bold, challenging, and yet achievable visions are important to those working together. They motivate and inspire others to perform at the highest level possible.

In 1987, former president of Notre Dame University, Father Theodore Hesburgh, had this to say about leadership and vision, "The very essence of leadership is that you have to have a vision. It's got to be a vision you articulate clearly and forcefully on every occasion. You can't blow an uncertain trumpet."

When the Dallas Stars won the Stanley Cup in 1999, the team often rallied around a cry of, "Find a way—Make a way!" No matter the situation, the team had crafted a vision of creating a positive outcome. They would find a way or make a way. It did not matter how. It just mattered that they got the outcome, that they reached the vision.

Achieving bold visions demands hard work and commitment. Yet, when you are around a good group of individuals, it is hard to accept anything else. Motivational genius Zig Ziglar likes to say, "You were born to win, but in order to become a winner you must plan to win and prepare to win. Then you can legitimately expect to win."

You will make your team more intelligent and you will win more often if you learn to articulate a compelling vision around what you are going to achieve.

All roles have positive and negative elements. In corporate management, for example, many of the positives have clear material gains associated with them. The fact is, salaries, bonuses, and stock options all tend to be significantly higher in the more senior roles, where time demands and pressures are greatest. It is, of course, the same in sports. Just look at head coaching salaries versus those of assistants.

Many roles also have perquisites (perks) that reflect the "power of the org chart." Often, special treatment is granted based upon where someone ranks in the organization. Although, authentic leaders develop a power that is anchored by the relationships they build and maintain.

There are also risks associated with positions of leadership. Intelligent coaches/managers communicate them to their potential leaders. Intelligent individuals, who do not want to face the risks of leadership, make a choice not to embrace those responsibilities.

Legendary Boston Celtic Larry Bird said, "People think it's an easy thing to be a leader. It's not. You have to earn the respect of your teammates. You have to be willing to challenge them as well as support them. And then you have to prove you are willing to do whatever it takes." So be it.

Over the years, my friend and National Hockey League coach Ken Hitchcock has learned to actually warn the leaders he is developing of the risks they will face. His challenge to them is to come into the role aware of what they will face. Here is a look at six points he has used over the past few years to communicate these risks. These are risks that leaders will face whether they are in the business world or competing in sports.

1. You will be watched constantly. Leadership is a fulltime job. You must be "on" twenty-four hours a day, seven days a week. You must continually conduct yourself in a manner that earns the respect of your teammates and coaches.
2. Trust and respect are extremely fragile. Earning your coach's respect and your teammates' trust takes a long time. It is a process that could take weeks, months, even years. One cutting remark, lie, indiscretion, or unethical act could destroy your credibility in an instant. Once trust and respect are gone, you cease being a leader.
3. You won't always be liked. As a leader, you will be put in situations and do and say some things that won't always be popular with all of your teammates. Your job is not to be the most popular person on the team. Your job is to do what is necessary and right.
4. You must deal with conflict. It will be virtually impossible to avoid dealing with conflict as a leader. Various conflicts will crop up between teammates and coaches over the course of a season, and you will need to manage and minimize them. There is always a risk that someone's

feelings will get hurt in the process—possibly yours. The best way to navigate through these tough issues:

a. Address issues early. Very seldom will they get easier to deal with.
b. Focus on the issue or behavior as opposed to the individual. It is not really the person you are upset with. It is their behavior.
c. Close on a positive. Express how the desired action or behavior will move everyone to a better outcome. Be as specific as possible.

5. You will be between a rock and a hard place. You may find yourself in some difficult situations between your teammates and your coaches. As a leader, you are expected to be the mediator between each of these groups. Each of them will have slightly different expectations and demands of you. At times, you will feel torn in different directions.

6. You might be disappointed. Finally, as a leader, you will be investing a lot of yourself in the success of the team. It feels great when you and your team reach your goals during the season. And conversely, it hurts deeply when you fall short. It's the risk that people take when they pour their heart and soul into any endeavor. You'll discover that taking risks and possibly falling short is much better than not taking the risk and living the rest of your life with regrets.

It seems clear that these issues will be faced by all leaders. Most readers already have or will soon deal with each of them. Equally important, the leaders you are developing within your organization will face them as well. However, I have found nothing more rewarding than being in leadership roles. My expectation is that you will either share this view currently or will quite soon.

It takes a serious commitment to succeed as a leader. It takes continuous improvement to be among the very best. An important leading indicator of success suggests that you are headed down this path. The fact that you are working to learn from material like this book demonstrates that you intend to excel as a leader. It further reflects that you will work to ensure the leaders you are building on your team will excel as well. I applaud your commitment of time and energy to these endeavors.

DEVELOPING
AND LEADING TEAMS

Developing and leading teams is the most rewarding work I can imagine. It is important. It is challenging. Developing yourself into an effective team leader demands a commitment to the team, a commitment to each individual on the team, and a commitment to continuous improvement. This should never be taken lightly. All of us have enough experience with poor bosses and coaches to know that not just anyone can do it well.

The impact of good leadership is undeniable. Both in terms of how it impacts results and the emotional impact it has on the people involved in the endeavor. Players and employees will certainly complain about a poor boss. Equally, they will extol the greatness of a good one. Players talk longingly about coaches who brought out the best of their capabilities. Often, it takes time to put the demands of a challenging leader in perspective. Yet, given that time, most participants are able to express the positive aspects of the experience. Leadership experts rightfully contend that a good leader compensates for a poor organization. Within the talent management doctrines of Texas Instruments, we used to say, "boss trumps company." That is, the quality of the supervisor was the number one factor in determining employee satisfaction and retention. Even if the entire company was struggling significantly, a good leader could hold their group together and deliver superior results. Likewise, poor leadership has very negative impact on a team, even when the larger organization may be performing well. The rewards of superior leadership and the associated team performance are tangible. Sound leadership improves bottom line results (winning) and morale. Simply said, it is good business. More importantly, it is honorable work.

You Can Improve

You can become a better leader! I have seen this happen over and over again throughout my career.

You can literally change the world with great teams. You can orchestrate a flood that impacts the world in ways that you are only beginning to imagine. Tolstoy once said, "Everyone thinks of changing the world, but no one thinks of changing himself."

Everyone can make changes that will improve their leadership performance.

Leadership Is Not a Birthright

Leadership is not something you were born with, although many believe this. Even our childhood stories of King Arthur or the presently popular *Lord of the Rings* trilogy reinforce elements of this flawed perspective. There is no checkmark for leadership on your birth certificate. While it is easier for some personalities, everyone can learn to become a better leader. You can learn how to motivate yourself and create an environment where others do the same.

It will take honest self-assessment and reflection to improve your performance as a leader and to be an important part of building great teams. It will certainly push you out of your comfort zone. Part of your learning will be make mistakes and learning by trial and error. Even armed with the most expertly applied principles, you will face unanticipated challenges. One of your greatest assets can be a genuine interest in what motivates and frustrates others.

Most importantly, this will be an ongoing process. Developing yourself as a great leader is something you can and will get better with over time. Simply reading a book like this reflects your personal commitment to improved team performance, and that commitment is what will lead you to improved leadership results.

Teamwork: It Is Everywhere

The world is full of failed companies and failed sports franchises with great individual talent. Great outcomes require individuals coming together and generating success as a team. You might contend that this is rather obvious in the business world and with team sports. But what about the individual sport participants (golf, tennis, etc.)? You might ask.

Even with the most individual sports, success in today's ultra-competitive environment demands a team approach. World-class performance places demands on the athlete, coach, agent, nutritionist, exercise physiologist, and more. Tiger Woods is clearly one of the most dominant athletes of our day. Yet, when you think of how Tiger recreated his swing in 2000, most likely you remember his swing coach Butch Harmon as well. And as 2004 turned to 2005, talk of new swing changes had Tiger linked to another great golf coach, Hank Haney. Tiger's Masters and British Open victories in 2005 were tangible proof that their teamwork was effective. Coach and player are working together to create a great outcome. It is the same for tennis, or ice-skating, or gymnastics. Great results demand a team-oriented focus, even for the most individual of competitors.

Nature rewards great team performance. Farmers learned centuries ago that teaming horses resulted in an ability to pull more weight than the same number of animals could pull individually. Further, they could get the stronger results with less wear and tear on the animals. Working collectively as a team, the horses could do more work for the farmer and deliver superior results.

Ducks and geese have evolved to demonstrate clearly that they can fly faster and further by working as a team. They fly in a distinctive "V" pattern and change leaders often. The sport of cycling has learned from this. While rewards are given to individuals, it is an ultimate team sport. Americans remember the championships Lance Armstrong secured, yet he could not have achieved them without extraordinary team performance. The team takes turns setting the pace, the team protects, the team attacks challengers, and the team is there for months of grueling preparation.

Many predators have learned that hunting as a team yields improved results. Pack hunting is relatively common and can yield exceptional results. By hunting with teamwork, there are prides of lions in Africa that have even learned to bring down the mighty elephant, a beast that outweighs the lion by twenty times.

Likewise, there are many examples in the business world of extraordinary individual craftsmen who have built successful enterprises. One of my favorite examples is that of the legendary guitar company PRS. Paul Reed Smith is one of the most likeable men in the world of music instruments. Part artist, part craftsman, part business executive, and fulltime visionary, Paul took his passion (to build a better guitar) and built a legendary company. What started as a one-man show has evolved into a global enterprise and a team focused on delivering a superior experience for the players who select their instruments. Paul's uncompromising focus on relationships and attention to any and everything that will make a difference in the instruments has been the key. While Paul brought an inspiring vision and a "roll-up-the-sleeves" energy, it has taken unmatched teamwork to build the kind of brand that PRS has become.

There are plenty of boutique shops and one-man companies that build a handful of guitars each year. Most are truly fine instruments. But Paul built a significant enterprise that employs a couple hundred people and builds thousands of instruments each year. There should be no confusion regarding the importance of Paul's vision, leadership, and impact. However, the company's lasting legacy will now be established by team performance.

Different Talent – Different Contributions

None of this should suggest that everyone will contribute equally. Differences in talent, experience, and energy alone mean dramatic differences in how much an individual contributes. This in no way, however, should diminish the impact that each person has on a team's success. After winning a gold medal in gymnastics in 1984, Mitch Gaylord's comments reflected this understanding. He summed up the U.S. team's performance like this, "A team championship doesn't happen because three people scored tens. It happens because all the guys score well. In my opinion, everyone deserved tens. We are all tens on this team!"

This is a great perspective and is equally applicable in the world of business. The challenges are so complex that it takes everyone contributing at a high level for the enterprise to be really successful.

There is an old story about two stonecutters who were

asked what they were doing. The first said, "I am cutting this stone into pieces." The second replied, "I am on a team that is building a cathedral." Which would you like to work with? Which would the owners of the cathedral want building their temple? Which will be most successful in their job and in life? Clearly, the second stonecutter understood his individual accountability to the team.

Self-Sacrifice

Nonetheless, there is something compelling about the self-sacrifice required to make a team successful. Sayings like "There's no I in team!" strike us as relevant for good reason. It is a sound way to reinforce the selfless honor of the team. Certainly, it resonates with the "common man." Also, reinforcing a sacrifice that might be made at the individual level, for the good of the team, makes sense. "There's no I in team!" is a nice balance to the kind of selfishness and excess that we are often immersed in.

Individual Power

It is very dangerous to understate the power of each individual in the group or to downplay in any way their individual responsibility to the team. If you ask members of your organization to give up their individuality, you are on a road to failure. They will start holding a part of themselves back. Once they start holding back, you are going to compromise team performance. You must get the most out of each and every individual. Even as you focus on intelligence, initiative, and integrity in the chapters coming up, you will need to do so with a focus on each individual as well as the collective team.

The children's game "Kerplunk" is a fascinating example of the old "straw that broke the camel's back." It reinforces the impact that each individual move has on the game's outcome. In the game, sticks are inserted all the way across a tube in a random fashion. Marbles are then inserted in the top of the tube. There are enough sticks crisscrossing through the tube to keep the marbles from falling. Players take turns removing sticks. Marbles shift and eventually begin to make their way all the way to the bottom of the tube. (Players do not want that to happen, as the player with the most marbles loses.) Often, the marbles fall to the bottom in large groups because a single stick changes the forces significantly when it is removed. Yet, was it really the single stick that caused the impact? Of course not. It was a cumulative effect. Each and every individual stick had an impact on the outcome.

In some respects, it is the same with rain that causes a flood. It is often said that no single raindrop considers itself responsible for the flood. But there is no flood without the cumulative effect of each raindrop. Through their "teamwork," the individual raindrops create a massive impact.

Even when we extol the greatness of the self-sacrifice required for the good of the team, we must do so with the recognition of how personal and individual this responsibility is. And certainly, the responsibilities of the leaders are the greatest. As such, we will spend a lot of time addressing important concepts from the leader's perspective.

People Power

Apart from the impact of education, process, technique, and technology, it is our people who are responsible for every important breakthrough, accomplishment, and victory.

Coaches live this every day. Great coaches have always gotten wonderful recognition for the results of their teams. John Wooden, Vince Lombardi, Casey Stengel, and Scotty Bowman are fondly remembered by both players and fans. Their greatness is routinely extolled in the public arena. Their greatness is anchored in having built the highest performing teams of their day. In today's world of salary caps and team parity, coaching that human talent is even more important. When Ken Hitchcock talks about achieving great results by getting improved results out of the individuals on the team, it makes perfect sense. Sports provide a perfect window into the competitive world of talent management.

However, in the world of semiconductors, isn't it the technology, not the people, that makes the real difference? As with many high technology industries it is quite true that we managed the smallest of details. Texas Instruments' chief technology officer, Hans Stork, liked to remind folks that, if an advanced semiconductor were the size of a football field, we would be controlling each individual blade of grass on the field. So obviously, in many industries, it is all about science and technology, not human resources. Right?

Quite wrong!

The competitive dynamics of the electronics industry prove that technological advantage simply can't be sustained. If it could, IBM would have no competition. Cisco would not exist. Redback, Hauwei, and a host of other networking competitors would never have spawned. Texas Instruments would have no real competition in the semiconductor industry. And on, and on.

Today's breakthrough is surpassed by someone else's tomorrow. The rate of improvement is staggering. The technological leads are held for only brief moments. Sustained superior performance requires much more than a mastery of chemistry and physics.

Even in situations where you are certain that the most essential element of success is the superior application of technology, or manufacturing might, or financial power, I challenge you to consider that it will be people who make it happen. It is our people who are responsible for every technological achievement, every discovery, and every decision. Whether in business or in sports, our human assets are the only sustainable advantage that we have.

What is a high performing team?

Ultimately, we have to be measured by results. Although it sounds harsh, a high performing team WINS! It is about winning games and championships. It is about winning market share and profitability battles.

Professional sports provide a stark look at this reality. Turnover in the coaching profession each year reinforces that employment and longevity demand success. A Peewee coach in your local community may actually be in the teaching business, but in the professional ranks it is a different story. A National Hockey League (NHL) coach is in the business of winning. Professional sports are a very distinct business. Testosterone, adrenaline, and hyperbole-laced to be certain, but business nonetheless. The only way to ensure your future is to win.

Success in the business world is not always on the public stage, but the expectation is quite the same. Your company grows and produces a profit or you don't have a job for long. The expectations are equally clear. Your continued employment and your quality of life are at stake. There are companies all over the globe just waiting to take your customers, and subsequently your livelihood, away from you.

I find it interesting to see how much attention business growth in Asia has gotten these past few years. The global viability of these companies and the regional strength is far from new. I made my first trip to Taiwan in 1986 and have traveled extensively in the region (including many trips to China) every year since. I have seen their commitment to winning on many fronts, in many industries and in many countries. My tenure at Texas Instruments brought me into contact with many industry leaders, both as customers and as competitors. I cannot imagine an enterprise that won't be impacted by global competition eventually, even if they aren't impacted today.

Texas Instruments crafted a strong technical position in the world of personal computing. Its team in Houston led the way toward portable computing. The early machines were far from today's sleek notebook computers and were more aptly described as luggable. Some of the key leaders in the business unit actually left and founded Compaq. Yet, Texas Instruments remained a force for many years. However, by the mid-1990s it was clear that we were far from best in class. Eventually, Texas Instruments sold the PC business to a Taiwanese electronics company, the Acer Group. They were better than Texas Instruments in this space. Acer had become quite a force in the world of electronics. They are known by many consumers around the world. However, when buyers chose an HP-Compaq, IBM, or Dell computer, they have likely selected a product with distinct and strong Asian connections as well. The percentage of notebook computers actually built (and increasingly designed by as well) by Compal and/or Quanta (both Taiwanese electronics giants) is staggering. With IBM's agreement to sell its personal computer business to Chinese electronics company Lenovo, we have another tangible example of global competitive front. It is not just isolated to computers. It is not just competition for manufacturing jobs. Competition around the world is global, and it is fierce.

When Cisco's CEO John Chambers talked about competitive threats, he spent more time talking about Chinese communications company Hauwei than he did Nortel. When Sony executives evaluate competitive threats, they focus more on Korea's Samsung than they do

RCA (which is now just a brand actually held by French conglomerate Thomson and whose TV business is now a joint venture with the Chinese company TCL) or Panasonic. When Nokia competes for cell phone business in China, they face not just names like Motorola or Sony-Ericsson that North American consumers know, but viable Chinese competitors such as Bird, Haier and TCL. The world really is smaller and more competitive than it has ever been.

The upside to all of this pressure to perform is that winning is a lot of fun. There is an ancient Japanese saying that I find compelling, "Many enemies—Great glory!" While I would not recommend that anyone seek out "Many enemies," the fact is most of us are destined to face significant and numerous challenges. Meeting those and succeeding in a highly competitive environment makes you feel good about what you have achieved. Just as there are no easy games on an NFL football schedule, there are no easy marketplaces to compete in for today's business leader. In any environment, if you intend to win, you must commit to superior team performance, and that performance depends on the leader.

Respected Team Leaders

NHL coach Ken Hitchcock uses a succinct, yet powerful, description for the role of leaders within his team. It is a good summary that merits our review.

Here are the Six Rs of Respected Team Leaders:

> 1. ROLE MODEL. All leadership begins with self-leadership. People will come to respect you only if you can walk your own talk and lead yourself effectively. You must be able to model the commitment, confidence,

composure, and character you expect from your teammates.

2. REMIND. As a team leader, you must continually remind your teammates about what is important—your common goal, your game plan, and your chemistry. Remind your teammates that all of the commitments and sacrifices they are making will pay off in the end.

3. REINFORCE. You will also spend a lot of time reinforcing the positive strides your teammates make. Be sure to compliment them often as a way to build their confidence and fuel positive momentum and a great environment on your team.

4. REASSURE. Because there are so many obstacles, setbacks, and adversities involved in every season, you will need to assure your teammates when they are feeling nervous, scared, frustrated, helpless, and hopeless. Give them a sense of hope and optimism.

5. REFOCUS. You will spend a lot of time helping your teammates refocus their negative thoughts on something more positive and productive. Shift their minds from the distractions and problems to workable solutions.

6. REPRIMAND. Last but not least, you must have the ability to constructively confront and reprimand your teammates when necessary. You must hold them accountable to live up to and maintain your team's rules and standards (especially on issues of integrity).

It is clear that superior team performance will be anchored by the contributions from your leaders. It is clear that your results will be improved through a disproportionate focus on the development of your leaders. Nonetheless, we can lift your organization's output by inserting more "I" throughout your organization. There are three unmatched and powerful "Is" that are essential and merit a more detailed review. Intelligence, Initiative, and Integrity will be the keys to your future success.

PART 1:
INTELLIGENCE

Making Your Team Smarter

Webster defines INTELLIGENCE as: "The ability to acquire and apply knowledge."

For great team success, intelligence is both a requirement and a key differentiator. Certainly, it starts with great mental power. There is no question that a high IQ will usually result in a distinct advantage.

In sports, it is often said that "a good big athlete will beat a good small athlete." It is accepted because of the consistent advantage that size brings (and it is so easy to see). Intelligence will bring a similar advantage. In the business world, a committed and smart worker will out-produce a committed worker. In sports, a smart and big athlete will be more valuable than a big athlete. As I like to remind my children, "The strong take from the weak, but the smart take from the strong."

Certainly, companies screen for academic performance when they recruit employees. Many use a grade point average (GPA) screen. It is a sound practice, as a strong academic performance is generally a reflection of raw intelligence and/or hard work. Both traits bring great advantage to the employer. It is not to suggest that work in the classroom is the only thing that counts and it can be outweighed by other characteristics and capabilities, but it is a good start. The most elite colleges recruit and admit based upon entrance exam test scores as well.

Interestingly, many sports teams are actually testing now (both for intelligence and personality profiles) before they draft. It is used because it works. You should commit yourself to search for and acquire the most intelligent resources and do not apologize for it.

However, the real question is, What can you do to make your team more intelligent? How do you make all the resources in your organization/team more intelligent?

The most operative word in Webster's definition is "apply." Intelligence has to be applied to really help the team. All of us have experienced the difference between individuals who are "book smart" versus "street smart." (Street smart implying the ability to really get things done.) There is also an important difference in being smart with game or business planning versus being smart on the field of play. There is value and a role for both. However, individuals who are smart on the field, in the heat of the battle, in the middle of the business deal, are the invaluable resources that carry the day. The best news is that there are ways to improve an individual's intelligence in such environments.

Let's start with some consideration of the difference between intelligence, instinct, and experience. I talked above about the importance of applying knowledge. Intelligence also suggests a need for continuous improvement as more knowledge is acquired. It further implies an element of effectiveness in being able to apply that knowledge.

Webster defines instinct as, "The innate, complex, and normally adaptive aspect of behavior."

Our friend Webster defines experience as, "Active participation in events or activities, leading to accumulation of knowledge or skill."

The good news is that Webster's definitions suggest you can improve your "instinct" with "experience." This also suggests, and rightfully so, that experience should increase intelligence; that you can accumulate the knowledge and make it innate. It can, and should be, the very best teacher. For many individuals, experiencing something is really the only way they truly learn and understand. Often, you have to let your team experience things firsthand to really raise their intelligence level.

On the other hand, it is frightening how many people repeat their mistakes. Some people get ten years of experience. Others simply get a year of experience and then repeat it ten times. Simply experiencing something does not mean you will really accumulate knowledge.

Here are five ways to make your team more intelligent:

1. Make sure your team members understand their roles. It is management's responsibility to communicate roles and to make sure they are understood.
2. Use tools. Write down their role as simply as possible. Use illustrations as necessary.
3. Communicate extensively. Talk to the individuals. Leave them written material. Review their role often.
4. Specify the outcomes that are to be achieved in the role. Make your expectations crystal clear. Talk in terms of results.

5. Work to help each individual see where their unique talents lie and how their specific role relates to the team's overall goal.

This is simple and essential. When you are taking these steps, remember what George Bernard Shaw said, "The problem with communication is the illusion that it has occurred."

If you do not have a clear role written down for everyone in your organization, if you have not made your expectations (outcome based) perfectly clear, you are not adding to your team's intelligence. If you are not prepared to do this, you are not serious about being a better leader and team builder.

Expectations

I have always been good about expressing my expectations. And, although I am highly verbal, I believe strongly in the value of having things written down as well. When I took over the Americas Sales organization in 1995, I came from having spent the last eight years in various business units. Although I started my Texas Instruments career in technical sales, to many folks I was an outsider. There was a lot of interest in what my perspectives were and where I would focus. My first meetings with sales offices around the country were all about expectations. I tried to establish extensive dialog about what I expected personally and what I expected out of our organization. I did it with specific material that clearly articulated my views. Likewise, in an interview for a company newsletter, I tried to steer the bulk of the conversation to be about expectations.

The foundation for team intelligence starts with a clear understanding of expectations.

It was essential that my direct reports have documented

specifics as well. The document shown below is a model for what I used (tweaked just slightly for each person) at that time. I created the outline shortly after I took over the Americas Sales organization. I had to modify it only slightly when I took over Worldwide Sales & Marketing at Texas Instruments in 1998. I made sure any new manager that joined our team got these written expectations early in our relationship. I used it each time we made a change and brought someone new into our team. It was specific. It was written down.

EXPECTATIONS

Let me start by addressing a few characteristics that I feel are critical. It should be a "given" that I expect the highest levels of personal integrity. Forthrightness, meeting personal commitments, and loyalty are extremely important to me. My personality provides little tolerance for sloppiness, tardiness, and missed deadlines.

Fundamentally, my primary expectations of your performance fall into four critical areas. They are teamwork, people development, strategy development, and tactical management/execution. Let me address each in further detail.

Teamwork
- Support the best interest of TI—balance your organizational needs with that of the total team.
- Be highly collaborative—willing to contribute and work in areas outside of your direct responsibility.
- Communicate and share best practices, identify issues for commonality.
- Develop effective team-oriented relationships with the Business Entities.

People Development

- Assess and develop talent.
- Spend lots of time with your top people.
- Set clear expectations and provide feedback on performance.
- Demand and reward excellence.
- Challenge your teams to consistently perform to their very best. (You not only get what you EXPECT but what you ACCEPT.)
- Dramatically improve or remove non-performers.
- Drive continuous improvement and constant learning throughout your organization.

Strategy Development

- Set and communicate key strategic priorities.
- Know your segment/area intimately—document and communicate a specific strategy.
  - Market/equipment, trends, and directions
  - Specific customer focus
  - Total Available Market to Total Imaginable Market (TAM to TIM) transition
- Develop and implement a plan to balance resources (e.g. Technical Sales Representative, Field Sales Representative, Account Managers, Regional Managers) across Segment/Area needs.
- Establish an evocative perspective that will help sell your strategies internally (secure Business Entity alignment and commitment).

Tactical Management/Execution

- Develop relationships with as many key "decision makers and influencers" (customers, distributors, educators/industry experts, Business Entity resources, etc.) as practical.
- Maintain key customer strategies as succinct working documents.
- Build a culture of strong customer advocacy.
- Drive assertively for profitable net revenue growth.
- Drive for Business Entity support when critical (effective internal selling). Evaluate risks, leverage internal capabilities, and win.
- Meet your forecast—explain major variances.
- Ensure that the most talented and highest contributing human assets are aligned with the most important assignments.
- Meet your forecast—explain major variances.
- Develop solutions when you identify problems—take the time to think through possible resolutions.
- Avoid surprises—communicate good and bad news quickly.
- Ensure that all written materials and communication reflect our commitment to excellence.
- Respond to required deadlines.
- Be cost conscious—drive for efficiency, as well as effectiveness.

In our sales organization it was essential to augment these "expectations" with very specific sales and market share expectations as well.

Feedback

Another essential (a simple and often under-utilized step) is to provide lots of performance feedback. Individuals must understand where they stand. As a leader in the organization, you have to provide specific and frequent feedback with regard to their performance.

If you are not providing routine and documented feedback to every person who reports to you and then subsequently ensuring that it is done throughout your entire organization, you are not serious about optimizing your organization's performance.

There are two important elements of feedback. The easy one, but one that is still often avoided, is to ensure that your organization embraces and uses a performance feedback process. For many folks this is the dreaded annual review. An annual review is not enough, but it is certainly a start.

What amazes me is that, even in a great company like Texas Instruments, I went many years without a formal review. Some supervisors just get very uncomfortable with the whole process. So they don't do it. Not every boss I had was a great role model for this process.

I started my post-college working days in the Bell System. When I was there, it might not have been the fastest-moving organization on the planet, but the parts to which I got exposed were disciplined. They convinced me that, if I expected continued employment, I would always make sure that everyone who reported to me got their performance review. It was non-negotiable, and I simply embraced it early in my career and stuck with it.

Yet, I admit that I did a poor job of ensuring that it took place everywhere in the Texas Instruments organization. Over the years, we have used any number of surveys to measure employee morale and satisfaction. However, by the mid-1990s, a practice that was once mandatory for the entire company had become voluntary, with each major organization deciding if, how and what they would survey. By the late 1990s, I had become convinced that we needed to consistently assess the satisfaction level of our folks in the sales organization. The new model we were using gave me great flexibility in how we approached the need. The book, *First Break All the Rules* by Buckingham and Coffman, influenced my belief that we needed to keep things very simple and provide some great guidelines on the kind of questions one should ask. Whether an individual understood what was expected of them at work and got performance feedback were at the top of the list of "must ask" questions.

As proud as I was of Texas Instruments' culture, our results in this area were not all that impressive. Almost a third of the respondents indicated that they were not clear on what was expected of them, and a slightly higher percentage indicated that they were not getting feedback on their performance. Wow! There were a lot of reasons that we were losing market share in the late 1990s, but I was convinced our own poor management performance was among them.

The great news about how we conducted the survey is that it was optimized for accountability. While it was anonymous to the individual level, it was tracked in minute detail, and we reviewed the results for every team in our rather large organization. There was nowhere to hide.

Over a two-year period of time, we took our score on an understanding of expectations to basically 100%. Nothing short of what it should have been, mind you, but I knew it was important progress nonetheless. We also got almost 90% of our respondents to acknowledge that they were getting feedback on their performance. Additionally, we worked with our leaders on the power of positive feedback, a lesson from the *First Break All the Rules* book. We doubled the percentage of folks feeling they had recently gotten some positive feedback from within the organization. Feedback that you give as quickly as possible after observing behavior is the most powerful. As we increased our attention to providing more ongoing and in-situ feedback, we improved our performance and raised the personal satisfaction of our work force.

I know that this concerted effort to improve our articulation of expectations down to the individual level and then to dramatically improve the quality of performance feedback is one of the reasons we were getting improved results. There were quite a few of important initiatives underway at this time as we worked to recover from our loss of market share. I know that this effort was one of the contributors to our organization's and our company's success. And I know our folks felt better about our work environment.

If you commit yourself to a disproportionate focus on expectations and performance feedback, you will improve your team's results!

Matching Roles and Talent

Matching roles to the talent available is certainly one of the most important things that managers and coaches do. There is massive variability in the expectations placed upon different roles. Think of a large corporation and the differences between the CEO and a line worker (plus hundreds of jobs in between). Each person has to be held accountable to know their role and to apply their individual capabilities to better the organization. The expectations that I wrote about so passionately have to be optimized for each role.

As the chief sales officer of Texas Instruments, my greatest exposure was "selling" to the many customers. For simplicity's sake, think of selling as: understanding the customer and their needs, developing a solution that meets the need, and securing a commitment from the customer to your solution. The ultimate objective was to build a relationship where our customers were consciously and systematically embracing our solutions. Although selling had been my domain, there were many people outside the sales force who had an essential role in selling to our customers.

Customers need to know they are important to the company. They want exposure to the business unit leaders who control development resources and manufacturing. In many cases the largest customers will want a personal relationship with the CEO. Their decision-making will be influenced by many individuals (all of whom are "selling" as a deal moves forward). However, few of the executives and business unit leaders really make great account managers. Listening to customers, assuring that your knowledge of the customer and their needs is greater than the knowledge of your solution, being a great customer advocate, dealing with rejection, and being persistent in pursuing new business demand different skills. It is a very distinct role. Finding and keeping the right kind of folks in these roles is essential to a company's health. There are some individuals with the skills and disposition to be great in many roles. I have found, however, that there is an even higher percentage who will contribute at the highest level when they are operating in a specific role matched to their capabilities and interest.

In the world of sports we get more visual reinforcement of the differences in roles. Linemen and running backs are both essential, yet almost exclusive. (Though I still remember fondly watching the Chicago Bears' "Fridge" (Perry) score a few touchdowns.) One of my first discussions of substance with Ken Hitchcock was about getting folks in the right roles and often the associated "battle" of getting them to accept what you needed from them. In 1999, when Hitch's Dallas Stars won the Stanley Cup, superstar Mike Modano was required to be a force from the "dots to the boards, on the face-off circle, and in transition." Jamie Langenbruner, in contrast, has to be an annoying and relentless physical presence everywhere on the ice.

Every player on your team must have a role. And certainly every role includes work ethic requirements in specific areas. The leader/manager/coach has to ensure that role is understood and the individual is being held accountable for the outcomes associated with the role. If individuals desire a different role, you must make sure it is earned.

Importance—Challenge—Control

Here is a piece of knowledge that you and your leaders can use to make your team more intelligent. There are three key fundamentals that your people want and need to perform their best for you.

1. Importance. They want a job that is significant. They want to create value. They want to do something that matters to their customers and company or organization. You'll need to explain how their role and their performance are doing just that.

2. Challenge. They want to be contributing in a manner that utilizes their skills. They want to be stimulated at work. They want to be stretched. Again, they will need feedback with regard to how they are meeting the challenge.

3. Control. They want to be empowered so they can make decisions about their work. They want enough control to be innovative. They want enough power to have some impact on how they do their work.

Continuous Improvement

My last point in this chapter on building team intelligence is what I call "raising the bar." By that I mean the process of continuous improvement.

There is no "stay the same" in business or in sports! It is like rowing upstream. You are making progress and moving ahead, or you are quickly sucked downstream.

Superior teams perform the best in the most difficult situations. For sports, the champions emerge from the teams that are playing the best at the end of the season. In business, superior teams reveal themselves when business conditions are most challenging. Especially at such times, top performers show a penchant for continuous improvement. At any point in time you can be assured that, even if you are not improving, some of your competitors are! Intelligent teams are driven to demonstrate continuous improvement.

In many respects, like accomplishing more by working as a group, continuous improvement is a natural state of life. Life evolves and changes because it is cosmically committed to survival. Whether by intelligent design, by divine intervention, or by random gesticulation, "life" has found it must grow and thrive to survive. It is always searching for ways to improve and assure its success and survival.

Every generation seems to believe that they are living in a period of unprecedented change. Maybe they are right. There has been discussion of this topic for centuries. Certainly at this point in human history there is an overwhelming array of material that talks about the power of change. There are books, DVDs, audiotapes, seminars, and speakers who specialize on the topic. The question to ask is, Do they address the key to success in a changing world? It is all about the power of continuous improvement.

If there is only one thing you should remember from this book, here it is, "To excel and thrive in a period of great change your rate of learning must exceed the rate of change." (Unattributed, but used by the author for 20 years now.)

Continuous learning is the key to continuous improvement. Intelligent teams focus on this. Great leaders find ways to keep raising the bar and improving the results.

My father (a high school dropout at the age of 16) reminded me often that what I learned after I thought I knew everything (about age 17, by the way) would make a real difference in my life.

Continuous learning is at the heart of continuous improvement. And continuous improvement is at the heart of building an intelligent and successful team.

If you are not constantly raising the performance bar and encouraging your team to constantly improve, you are not serious about building great teams!

SUMMARY: THE THREE BEST WAYS TO BUILD TEAM INTELLIGENCE

1. Make Your Expectations Clear (role assignments—expectations—outcomes)
2. Provide Lots of Performance Feedback
3. Keep Raising the Bar (focus on continuous learning and improvement)

PART 2: INITIATIVE

The Engine, Ensuring Your Teams Take Action

Webster defines INITIATIVE as: "The power, ability, or instinct to begin or to follow through energetically with a plan or task."

While anchored with a view of beginning a task, Webster clearly expresses initiative as an ultimate measure of getting something done. A Ferrari is a beautiful car, for example. It is a stunning, high performance machine! However, without fuel and a driver to take some initiative, it has little real value.

One of my favorite views is an expression invoked extensively in hockey circles, "Hard work will beat talent if talent doesn't work hard!"

This is a quote I first heard from Ken Hitchcock in 1999. For me it was a first. I went straight from my coffee meeting with Hitch and wrote it on my whiteboard. The quote stayed visible in my office until the day I retired from Texas Instruments. I think it sits at the heart of superior team performance, and it screams of the importance of initiative!

"Hard work will beat talent if talent doesn't work hard!"

If there is a single takeaway that will improve your organization/team's performance from this section of the book, that statement might well be it. Teams without hard work simply do not win. It is too competitive in the worlds of business and professional sports to sustain success without extraordinary initiative from individuals on the team. Success is not ordained from above. I believer, however, that it does come from our glands. "Sweat glands," that is.

A Commitment to Work

Hard work is the natural byproduct of commitment. Mature individuals realize that, when they commit themselves to achieving a specific goal, they may well put in a lot of blood, sweat, and tears to turn their dream into a reality.

But to reach a goal and win, you have to build a team. Building that winning team demands a commitment to put in the necessary work. Teams that have a culture of taking initiative are self-motivated. While the role of the leader is essential in setting the pace, the organization and its members do the work on their own. They must take initiative and show an individual commitment to their development, training, improvement, diet, rest, etc. The leadership has to reinforce how these efforts are part of a long-term plan to achieve the dream. And the leadership has to demonstrate this initiative.

In most cases, others in the organization will admire the leader's commitment and be motivated to follow such initiative. However, not all individuals will react this way. Some less committed coworkers may even attempt to sabotage the leader's efforts. They may ridicule the efforts or even attempt to embarrass those setting the pace by suggesting that they are making others look bad. Not everyone automatically embraces the commitment and work ethic required to win. You and your leadership face a formidable element of human nature where laziness, jealousy, and mediocrity might well reveal itself. You must take a stand and reinforce and reward the elements of initiative, hard work, and commitment.

Basketball legend Michael Jordan said, "The second I let down, particularly if I'm perceived as the leader of my team or my company, I give others an opening to let down as well." Why not? If the person out front takes a day off or doesn't work hard, why should anyone else?

Folks like Michael Jordan believe in setting the example because it works. It is another difficult demand of leadership. However, that is just the way it really is.

Texas Tech basketball coach Bob Knight was once quoted as saying, "The hardest thing about climbing the ladder of success is fighting your way through the crowd at the bottom."

I view that as his way of saying you have to take the initiative to get started and that once you got started it might not be as tough as you think. There is an old saying, "You can't climb the ladder of success with your hands in your pockets." Either way, these quotes suggest that you have to take action, you have to get to work. You are not going to magically become successful. Your teams won't magically win. You can't meet and exceed high expectations without concerted effort.

There is an old but engaging book on management, *Managing*, by Harold Geneen. Geneen was the leader who created the multi-billion-dollar diversified ITT empire. At one time, their holdings spanned across a major communications company, defense electronics, and hotels and casinos. At the risk of over-simplifying Geneen's book, his strongest message is that you will have to work very hard and make sacrifices to achieve the kind of success he achieved. You will need the support of your family and a lot of people in your organization.

Success at the very highest level may not be for everyone, simply because everyone can't put forth and sustain the kind of effort that will be demanded.

I could not agree more. My friend Ken Hitchcock knows that being a successful head coach in the NHL, or at any level in any field, requires a commitment of time and energy that is hard on the golf handicap and the family. Likewise, being an executive in the fast-paced, technically challenging world of semiconductors (or almost any business for that matter) takes a commitment and a road schedule that only a coach can appreciate.

Work—Life—Balance

In the fall of 2005, I was at a BTS client conference discussing executive education. BTS is an executive education and development consultant. They are domain experts when it comes to the world of business simulations. I once heard their executive vice president Dan Parisi say, "You don't learn to fly a plane these days without the use of a simulator. You shouldn't try to run a global business without simulation-based education as well." I could not agree more. And if you were looking to build a business simulation around key principals, I can't imagine a better group to work with than BTS.

The point is that there was a group of business and training/development executives at this conference. At one point the dialog turned to the need for work/life balance. Frankly, I found myself amused. The kind of balance these folks were fantasizing about just does not exist in the ultra-competitive world of global businesses. Leaders who think they can get by on a 30-40 hour work week won't have much of an enterprise to lead for long. The day the executives at Cisco find themselves working at that pace is the day that China's Huawei will take their best customer.

What the average worker calls work/life balance simply does not exist for today's top leaders. That is not to say you can't have a fulfilling life on many fronts. You can make your family important and share grand experiences together. You can be active in some charitable endeavors. You can work to maintain mental, physical, and spiritual balance. However, it won't be easy. You will need a solid support group (family and friends), a very strong sense of prioritization, an ability to say "no" occasionally, and a capacity for hard work.

I tried to start this book by reinforcing how important and rewarding your work as a leader should be. I am not changing the story. I am simply reinforcing the importance of acknowledging that it takes hard work and that the leader must set the pace. Again from the great Zig Ziglar, "You don't pay for the price for success, you enjoy the benefits of success."

He is quite right, yet you will work hard along the way to earn those benefits..

The Knowing—Doing Gap

Jeffrey Pfeffer, a professor of organizational behavior at Stanford, has conducted some extraordinary work around what he calls "the knowing—doing gap." His book, *The Knowing—Doing Gap: How Smart Companies Turn Knowledge Into Action* (Harvard School Press, 2000), offers a detailed look at this topic.

At the risk of vastly over-simplifying his compelling perspectives, the title of the book says a lot. There is an enormous difference between knowing what the right thing to do is and really taking that action.

Even if your team is intelligent, that will be far from enough to win. Intelligence, unless it is applied, simply does not matter much when it comes to building a winning team. You really begin to operate on a difference performance plane when you (as a leader) and your team take action as opposed to simply knowing what should be done.

The Power of Speed

"Speed Kills," and usually it kills the competition. I've heard coaches claim for years that "You can't coach speed." In some respects that is true from a theoretical point. However, theory won't win championships and undisputed market share leadership. The more salient point is that a team that acts fast has an advantage.

Fast and violent usually defeats slow and perfect. And initiative (taking the action) is the very first reflection of speed!

Combining the demand for speed with the concept of "the knowing—doing gap" reminds me of a success story inside Texas Instruments. Their Digital Light Processor (DLP) business is very important to the company and very high profile. DLP systems are most often found in high-end televisions and digital projectors (portable for business applications and large systems for digital cinema). In the mid to late nineties Samsung was the dominant customer for DLP systems in televisions. It was essential that Texas Instruments develop a broader customer base.

One important target was Thomson/RCA. Although they lacked a product portfolio that targeted the high end of the market (where DLP in HDTV was most attractive), they clearly had the brand presence to help our stature in Europe and with the broader market in North America. Thomson/RCA had invested early in a technology that competes with DLP. As such, progress with the account was slow. Further, Texas Instrument's DLP business unit was not sure how much they really needed the engagement.

Fortunately, the account manager felt differently. He was motivated (both financially and emotionally) to find a way to secure a significant base of business with Thomson/RCA. At a critical juncture in the ongoing dialog, this account manager picked up the speed of the interaction and called for reinforcements. His every instinct told him that we had to get more senior management engaged with the account and that we had to show more definitive interest in having them as a customer. "We had to show them more love."

He immediately moved to get me (as the chief sales officer) more involved. He requested that Texas Instrument's CEO rearrange his schedule to facilitate a meeting at the upcoming Consumer Electronics Show. He told the customer that Texas Instruments was eager to find a way to secure a major engagement and the reflection of our commitment was the attention our most senior executives were showing.

This account manager was action oriented and was showing urgency. He did not have a well-expressed written strategy for the engagement. What he had was a commitment to winning the business. Within a few months we had our first real program with Thomson/RCA. Although Thomson/RCA was far from Texas Instrument's largest DLP customer, it has proven to be important and opened the door to even further system level engagements in multiple product areas. It also prompted Thomson/RCA to stop development of TVs with the competitive technology.

This particular account manager is not Texas Instruments' most impressive presenter or developer of written account strategies. In fact, during account reviews we conducted a few years ago, his performance was in the bottom half. But the essential element is that he was getting great results. And, not only was he winning at Thomson/RCA, but as soon as we put him on an additional account, we began to secure a significant increase in our business with that customer as well.

As former Chinese party chairman Deng Xiaoping once said, "Black cat or white cat, if it catches the mouse, it is a good cat!"

Take Initiative With Passion And Enthusiasm

Great teams and their leaders display tremendous passion and enthusiasm. The more you bring passion and enthusiasm to your initiatives, the more successful you and your teams will be. As a leader by example, it will be your job to bring energy to your organization. This enthusiasm is highly contagious. You have to show your love for your business to your coworkers.

Successful teams learn to enjoy the challenge of preparing to win. In sports that is the daily grind of practice. In the business world that is often the daily grind of putting out your product or the months of work required to close a big sale. It is about enjoying the journey, not just the destination. Great leaders come to work with a smile on their face, ready to work hard.

Make no mistake, sports and businesses are impacted by momentum. When the energy level is down within the team, the leaders have to get things cranked back up. Passion and enthusiasm can do just that. Passion and enthusiasm multiply the power of your initiative, and they will yield a big advantage to any endeavor in which you compete.

Let Your Initiatives Instill Your Will

Vince Lombardi is generally recognized among the finest coaches ever and a constant builder of winning teams. He captured the importance of this concept when he said, "The difference between a successful person and others is not a lack of strength, not a lack of knowledge, but rather a lack of will."

Here is another story Ken Hitchcock loves to share with his

leaders about Michael Jordan. Dehydrated and dizzy because of food poisoning and a stomach virus, Jordan still carried the Chicago Bulls to a game five win over Utah (on their home court) in the 1997 NBA playoffs through his sheer competitiveness and strength of will. He could barely stand. Yet, Jordan put the Bulls on his back playing 44 minutes and scoring 38 points, including the game-winning 3-pointer in the final seconds. Said Bull's teammate Scotty Pippen, "I've never seen Michael as sick as he was, to the point where I didn't think he was going to be able to put his uniform on. The effort he came out and showed us was incredible. He's not only the greatest player ever, but he's the greatest leader ever."

Former Detroit Pistons great Isaiah Thomas felt the same way about the power of will, "Basketball is less a battle of skill and more a battle of wills." Of course, it takes great skill and intelligence to win, but it takes initiative anchored with relentless will power as well.

You and your top leaders have to be committed to winning. If winning were not important, why would you or anyone else be willing to invest so much of yourselves to achieve it. For most leaders, losing is simply not an option. Great leaders seem able to virtually will their teams to victory. It might be a big play (or closing a big sale) at a crucial moment to spark your team. It might be keeping everyone focused on the essential tasks at hand as the competitive pressures are highest. In all cases, it is reflected in a "refuse to lose" mentality.

Initiative "quick hits":

- **Lead, follow, or get out of the way!**
- **Step up or step aside!**
- **Go hard or go home!**

There is no shortage of these, because the concept is so important to wining teams. Your leaders will know this and will work to impose their will on their teammates. You and your top leaders must make every effort to get everyone on board. You must also be willing to go it alone when necessary!

New York Yankee Jason Giambi said, "A leader doesn't have to be the best player on the team, but he has to care about winning."

And from Ralph Waldo Emerson, "For the resolute and determined there is time and opportunity!"

If you are not reinforcing the importance of speed and taking initiative within your team, you are not really serious about superior team performance.

Results

Success demands that you focus on the results that really matter. The biggest danger in talking about initiative is creating an organization that only believes that a great effort is enough.

A great effort is a great effort, but it is NOT enough. You have to focus on end results that lead to winning!

In 1995 when I returned to a sales leadership role at Texas Instruments, I quickly built a candid and enjoyable relationship with one of our new distribution account managers. We had asked this young man to come in from a field-based account management role and work in a more corporate environment, directing our efforts to sell more effectively through one of our major distributors. It is a good development role for regional sales managers, and we felt this individual had solid potential. Because our distribution network is essential to our selling results, these roles get a lot of exposure to the vice president of sales position that I was in.

Now this particular guy was confident and ambitious. He

missed no opportunity to discuss his career expectations and outlook. And like most of us he was concerned about how much he earned. One of the first lessons I tried to teach him was that we were going to reward him based upon his results, not his potential. His potential got him into certain roles, but the big payoffs would only come with exceptional results. Many times I reminded him (and many others, before and after him), "We pay for results, not potential."

Although I got that particular principle right, I also made one of my biggest mistakes about that same time. After over eight years in operational roles, I found myself trying to find and implement leading indicators for sales results. It is an interesting idea in theory, but my problem was that I was willing to measure these leading indicators extensively and even pay bonus dollars for them. My organization figured out how to hit these metrics and yet we lost market share. People were hitting their objectives, getting impressive bonus payouts, and yet the company was under performing. It was not a good situation.

The simple answer was to get the sales force back to only being measured on net revenue and market share. Yes, there were important early indicators that we needed to track, but at the end of the day it was only net revenue that mattered. If our work did not result in net revenue gains, it probably was not the right kind of work.

Although our company was doing many things differently to improve our performance, I am certain that our simplified net-revenue-based performance metrics were an important catalyst for improved results. You simply can't get away from the fact that we started a run-of-market-share gains that, as of 2006, was working on five consecutive years. We focused on the results that really mattered, and it was clearly improving our performance.

Decisive Action

The best teams have leaders who are quick to take action. They build a culture where the key objectives (expectations) and key principles to be embraced are extensively communicated. But they must also allow their resources (the team) the flexibility to take action in the heat of the battle. Leadership among the teams who win the most know they can't possibly predict everything that will happen. They work to build a culture where initiative is expected of everyone.

The best-performing organizations also spend little time worrying about what more senior management or coaches will think when they face a requirement for decisive action. They act! Striving for great, not just good, is anchored with initiative.

Nineteenth century lawyer and politician William Jennings Bryan had a great view on creating your destiny, "Destiny is not a matter of chance; it is a matter of choice. It is not a thing to be waited for; it is a thing to be achieved."

Alabama football coaching legend Bear Bryant loved to say, "Be good or be gone."

Both compelling views ask us to take things into our own hands. You can create your own destiny, but it will start with initiative.

Mistakes

I hate mistakes!

I hate watching them get made. I hate being a part of them. I don't particularly like correcting them, and I certainly hate making them myself. Yet, I have made a ton of mistakes in my career. I could fill chapter after chapter of the strategic, tactical, and human development-related mistakes I have made. I do not like mistakes in the least, but I have learned that they are inevitable. Initiative-oriented individuals and organizations make mistakes! As a leader, as a builder of great teams, you will have to learn to live with the fact that mistakes are made.

That is not to say, however, that you have to accept mistakes. What you have to do is correct mistakes and move on. You have to acknowledge that they are going to happen. You have to make it clear that a quickly corrected mistake can still get you closer to a favorable outcome. In no way would I ask you to abandon a personal quest you have for perfection. If you are feeling that bold, I will only applaud your confidence and commitment. My counsel is simply to suggest that you will experience your fair share of mistakes, even if you don't make any yourself; and if you can build a team that accepts their inevitable nature and quickly takes action to correct them, you will be on your way to better results.

I have harsh memories of my first failed test in college. It was the first and only time I would fail an exam. During my sophomore year I was taking a linear algebra class. I had already completed three courses (15 credit hours) in calculus and two courses of differential equations (8 credit hours). I had gotten an A or B in each of those classes. I was confident in my math skills and probably approaching this new material (matrix math/linear algebra) a bit too casually. When it came time to study for the first exam, I reviewed many of the homework problems we had completed during that period. The problem was that I did not really redo any of the problems. I looked over the work I had previously completed; and because I felt I understood precisely what was on the paper, I assumed I really knew the material.

The real problem was that I simply recognized the work on the page was correct. I was not really reinforcing the skill of completing the task; I was simply reinforcing that I could recognize when it was right.

When it came to test time, I was poorly prepared. I did not spend enough time doing the work. If the professor had come over and started doing the work, I could have "recognized" it, but I could not do it. I failed that exam!

I never again fell into the recognition trap. When it came time to reinforce my knowledge base, I would do it by completing the work start to finish. It was tough to overcome a failed (F) test at the college level, but I ended up hammering the two additional tests we had in the course and did well on the final. The outcome: a solid B+ that I earned by correcting my mistake.

I was a part of a few mistakes at Texas Instruments that stand out as well. In the mid-'90s, the dial-up modem market was becoming a very significant market space for semiconductors. Chicago-based U.S. Robotics had become one of Texas Instrument's largest customers for digital signal processors. Our revenue with U.S. Robotics had screamed to a peak of two hundred million dollars per year.

However, the market had become very competitive. One of our top rivals had targeted the space and had targeted this account. To make a long story short, they were developing a more complete solution. We were tackling the challenge in a very discrete fashion, and they were applying their best technology in system level solution. We took the relationship with U.S. Robotics for granted. We thought they would accept the Texas Instruments solution because of our history and give us time to develop a more competitive, more integrated, and lower cost solution.

When our account came to explain why we were losing a major program, they made it clear that they felt we had not applied our most compelling technology and capabilities to solve their solution. They suggested that, if we looked at their problem like we did in the cellular handset space, we would long ago have delivered a more integrated and lower cost solution.

As the market evolved from dial-up modems to digital subscriber line (DSL) and cable modems, we did so with a commitment to compelling, integrated, system-level solutions. We were not going to repeat the mistake we made with U.S. Robotics. And we didn't.

I also remember a time when one of my key development managers tried to resign after a major failure on a high profile technology/product development program. At this point in my career, I was new to advanced technology development. Fortunately, I had an experienced design and development team. This team was working to develop the first one-micron feature size, very high speed, military static RAM memories.

Excitement was high as we began studying the latest version of our products. However, we quickly learned that the devices were not functional enough to move toward official qualification and production release. The development leader indicated that we had missed some fundamental issues during simulation (still in the design stage before we were actually producing them). His perspective was that it was a clear mistake that could and should have been avoided. He knew the error had cost us precious time and probably three to five hundred thousand dollars in development costs. He thought he should step down from the role.

I was frustrated and disappointed, but I saw things differently. I wanted to know if we were learning things that would help us in the future. I wanted to know if the mistake could be avoided in the future. I wanted to know how quickly we'd be ready to move forward with a new design. I then explained that Texas Instruments had made a half-million-dollar investment in this leader and his team, and we could not afford to walk away from that.

If you are taking action, mistakes are going to be made. So be it. Correct them and move forward.

SUMMARY: THE THREE BEST WAYS
TO ENSURE TEAM INITIATIVE

1. Reward Timely Action (focus on Speed).
2. Reward Results Versus Effort (pay for performance versus potential).
3. Build A Culture Where Corrected Mistakes Are Acceptable And Acknowledged As Inevitable.

PART 3:
INTEGRITY

Establish Soul Or You're Lost In A Deep Hole

Webster defines INTEGRITY as, "Firm adherence to a code or standard of values."

Integrity is the glue of lasting organizations and teams. In many respects, integrity can be thought of as a quality metric for your organization. Unfortunately, it is often most obvious when it does not exist. However, the power of uncompromising integrity must never be underestimated. Integrity may well be the most important "I" in team.

Samuel Johnson (1709-1784) was arguably one of the most important English writers of the eighteenth century. Since I have been reinforcing the importance of intelligence and initiative earlier in the book, I am certain he would counsel us now with a wise insight on integrity and its importance. "Integrity without knowledge (intelligence) is weak and useless, and knowledge without integrity is dangerous and dreadful."

Over the past few years, it seems that a lack of integrity sits at the heart of many of the corporate issues that have garnered national attention. Whether it is the examples at Enron, Tyco, or others, it causes me to cringe when I personally see the arrogance and lack of integrity reflected in the decisions made by the key leadership of these companies. As a senior executive, it embarrassed and angered me to learn of the mismanagement and reckless compromises they seem to have made. I hope you feel a sense of anger as well, because it will help you avoid ever getting in a similar situation.

Integrity is a Habit

Integrity requires a constant focus. Its importance must be acknowledged twenty-four hours, seven days a week. Two thousand years ago, Greek scholar and philosopher Aristotle said, "Quality is not an act. It is a habit." Make no mistake, integrity is precisely the same! If something is a habit, then you are obviously doing it every day. It is the normal way you conduct yourself and your business.

Quality standards can't change due to schedule pressures. Businesses can't adjust their quality standards to the calendar. If a product is a failure early in the month, it must be a failure late in the month when you are fighting to meet the quarter's revenue commitment. Integrity must be viewed precisely the same way.

I am not talking about moral questions per se. I do not judge my organization or my peers by their religious convictions, marital choices, political leanings, etc. Those are very personal in nature and, provided they do not impact the organization's performance, I stay away from them. When they impact the organization is the key decision-making criteria here.

Here is a good set of questions to ask yourself:

Is it impacting the customer?

Is it impacting the other employees?

Is it impacting the shareholder-company?

If it is, then leadership must step in immediately!

Likewise, when attempting to resolve issues, you can ask what is fair to those three powerful constituents (customers, employees, shareholders).

The more public your position, the more relentless and demanding is the call for integrity. Make no mistake: there are people out there who want you to fail.

A failure of integrity is likely to generate more external attention and emotion than failures of intelligence or integrity. Operating from a base of unquestioned integrity is arguably the greatest gift you can give yourself. Football coach Vince Lombardi had a great quote about quality and excellence, "The quality of a person's life is in direct proportion to their commitment to excellence, regardless of their chosen field or endeavor." Based upon everything we know about Lombardi, it seems certain that this must include an excellence of integrity as well.

You will have to articulate your expectations in this area quite clearly. Do not leave room for interpretation. Commit time to address these very important issues. Make your expectations clear and hold yourself and the organization accountable to meet them.

Do you care?

Being a part of something bigger than yourself is one of the most rewarding elements of team performance. The path to greatness is so demanding that you simply must enjoy the journey. That journey is best shared with people you care about.

Great teams care about one another. Great teams give extra effort because they care about their shared success. The bonds are strongest among teams that operate with the highest adherence to a set of values (i.e. high integrity). They care about one another; they protect the value of the team; they balance the demands of customers/fans, teammates, and shareholders/ownership. They do it consistently, and they win!

A commitment to the group/team really is an issue of integrity. This is where all the team talk of commitment and self-sacrifice comes from. While you need every member to excel in their role, you also need each of them to reflect a commitment to the team. When the team has individuals that are putting themselves before the organization, they have yet to become a real team; and they will not win consistently.

In professional sports it is reflected in teams that look great on paper or have individuals with incredible personal statistics, yet they do not win championships. In the world of business the most striking failures are reflected in the unparalleled egos of leaders who corrupt company financials for personal gain.

There is no shortage of individuals who claim an unwavering commitment to victory. There are many who declare that they want to be the very best. Yet, few seem to really understand the price that must be paid to achieve greatness. Talking about a commitment to winning, yet not acting in that manner, is an issue of integrity. If your team is not willing to prepare to win and not performing in a manner that will secure victory, do not let them embrace visions of greatness. You have to keep the team grounded in the current state and focused on the small steps in the journey that will build a culture of winning. Focusing on the "victory" itself, without securing the effort required to bring it, is disingenuous.

Essence Versus Image

Denny Van Avery is an executive coach. He is a compelling character who reflects intelligence, initiative, and integrity in all that he does. Denny coaches his clients on the need to be "authentic." His challenge to you would be to manage from your essence and character, not from personality and image. His advice is sound. And it allows you a great deal of freedom in terms of how you operate. It simply demands that you behave as who you really are. Your shareholders, your coworkers, your teammates are too smart for you to hide behind something that is not genuine. Operate differently and you will be violating an issue of integrity.

With all the material available and intended to improve your performance as a leader (this book included), it is tempting to try and fit a particular model. Don't think it will work. You cannot be true to anyone else or to any organization if you are not true to yourself.

The one issue upon which there is no compromise is that you must set the example. The leadership will be constantly evaluated by the organization. Zig Ziglar once claimed that his "momma" said, "If you set the example, you won't have to set many rules." There may be no better advice when it comes to building winning teams or raising children.

I always liked to remind my leaders that their people will not pay that much attention to what is said. The organization will determine what is important and what is valued based upon the metrics that are tracked and where the leadership spends its time. Everyone observes the leadership. You have to set the example! And you have to commit time to this topic. If you can't, don't let yourself get into a leadership role.

Know Thyself

Dr. Joyce Brothers offers some sound advice when she says, "You cannot consistently perform in a manner which is inconsistent with how you see yourself."

This will be true for you and for your leadership and for every member of your team. You and your team will have to meet the challenges you face in a manner that is consistent with your character, not some image you are trying to attain.

College basketball's legendary coach John Wooden's advice is similar, "Be more concerned with your character than with your reputation. Your character is what you really are while your reputation is merely what others think you are."

A Compass For Authenticity

Operating from a position of the highest integrity demands that we meet the challenges we face with a "personalization process." It will not be the same for everyone. You have to find a way to put a spin on the objectives that truly match your essence.

This starts with knowing what you really want and expect from yourself. You cannot effectively lead others until you come to terms with yourself. You cannot lead in an authentic fashion until you get brutally honest with yourself. If you can address your most personal objectives in this manner, you set the stage for exceptional results.

I have always been a real believer in the power of purpose and vision statements. They can do wonders for putting focus on your objectives and priorities, both personal and professional. Done with uncompromising awareness of self, they lay the foundation for operating from essence versus image.

It is generally accepted that businesses and sports teams operate most effectively when they have clear objectives set. Vision statements have become mainstream for almost all businesses operating today. (Though I'll not embarrass anyone with a look at how confusing many can be.) A strong case can be made for the value of vision statements for individuals as well.

Having a vision and purpose statement is highly personal. I would not encourage you to share your specifics publicly. That said, for credibility purposes, I will share mine. I have shown it to individuals in a private setting many times in the past, but this is the first time I have taken it into the public domain. Nonetheless, I believe in the vision statement's power and feel it is essential to share. I have watched it impact folks I work with many times. Generally, I would share it only when I felt someone was really struggling with fundamental issues of commitment and prioritization at work. My contention is that, with a documented vision and purpose statement, you have a tool to help you set your priorities and boundaries.

I wrote my first vision statement back in 1980. I refine it occasionally, but it is interesting how little it has changed over the years. My thinking starts with a list of characteristics I strive to reflect, moves to a purpose statement, and then transitions to a more classic vision statement.

Characteristics:
>Loving husband and father
>Healthy and happy
>Committed to getting the most from my capabilities
>Continuous learner, constantly improving
>Ethical, fun, and fair
>Authentic, managing from essence/character as opposed to image/personality. (Yes, I included this element after engaging with the aforementioned Denny Van Avery.)

Purpose Statement

    To assist and inspire others to achieve the most from their capabilities and to reach the highest levels of personal satisfaction.

    To leave a lasting mark on the business landscape, primarily through the development of human talent.

Personal Vision Statement

    To be key member of the most senior management of a company committed to being the best in the world in their targeted field. I expect to always operate in a culture of high business ethics, a commitment to deliver superior value, innovative products and services, a value of strong external views, of profitability, and of being fun and fair.

For those who might not know too much about Texas Instruments, I will only suggest that having spent the vast majority of my career with this fine company it is quite consistent with my vision statement.

The High Integrity Attitude

Having the right attitude is an element of operating with uncompromising integrity. It is an important part of adhering to an appropriate code. Of course, often we don't make it clear when we ask folks to bring a good attitude.

Most managers and coaches believe that employees who are positive, cooperative, enthusiastic, and supportive are stronger contributors. There is little question that most people prefer to be around others who enjoy their work.

However, it is certainly more than being happy about your

work. "Management's" interest is really in your performance, in the results you attain. I have already expressed the importance of being true to yourself. Not everyone is the same positive, bubbly, outspoken individual. Nor do they need to be. It is how your attitude shows itself in terms of accomplishments that counts in both business and sports.

The request for a great attitude is more specifically a request for being dedicated, determined, optimistic, enthusiastic, positive, and cooperative. Virtually all of us would like to be described this way. More importantly, such traits really are within almost everyone's grasp. We each own and control our attitude. This can't be stressed enough. You control your own attitude. We do not control every situation, and we certainly can't control every outcome, but we can control how we approach and respond to it.

Norman Vincent Peal once said, "Any fact facing us is not as important as our attitude towards it, for that determines our success or failure."

Even in a world filled with massive global competition, there will always be a demand for people dedicated and enthusiastic about their work. I can also assure you that your attitude is as contagious as the flu. Each of us should consistently ask ourselves if our attitude is worth catching.

Creating an environment where you expect your team/ organization to reflect dedication, determination, and enthusiasm and holding them accountable for such is an issue of integrity.

Rely On Yourself

You become vulnerable to issues of integrity when you begin relying too much on others for praise. It is essential that you rely on yourself for confidence. Certainly, public recognition from others can give your confidence a "jump-start." And it is not all bad. The key, however, is not to use external praise as a primary source of confidence.

Because of the public nature of professional sports (TV coverage, the written press, fan adulation, etc.), Ken Hitchcock has always counseled his players not to put much stock in the praise of others. Why? There are two primary reasons. First, sustainable confidence comes from within (it is authentic). You don't want to rely on other's opinions of you to determine your level of confidence. This is entirely outside of your control. Second, you might often be in an environment where praise is not given very often. If you need other people to give you confidence, and the person who is leading you is not giving any, your confidence will starve to death. Take your confidence form your preparation, your known strengths, and your past success.

When you worry too much about what others think, you become vulnerable as well to manipulation and exploitation. It is a selfish trait that may cause you to put your organization or teammates at risk. You risk performing in a manner that is inconsistent with the code of conduct demanded to make the full team successful. As such, you risk violating issues of integrity.

Optimism Builds Integrity

Confidence and optimism allows individuals to avoid compromising on issues of integrity. And those pressures to make shortcuts, to cheat, to do anything to win will be greatest following defeat.

The current steroid controversy in baseball is certainly an issue of integrity. We contend, if those players involved had more authentic confidence in themselves, they would be inordinately less willing to compromise the integrity of the game to secure a victory. In cheating, they compromise their personal integrity and that of the game. It cannot bring an outcome that ultimately benefits them or their fans.

Another important way to demonstrate your integrity and confidence is how you react to failure. How do you respond when you make a mistake? Do you give up? Do you make a list of excuses? Or do you learn lessons from the mistakes, refocus on the next challenge, and correct your mistakes? Confident individuals (athletes, business professionals, coaches, etc.) don't like making mistakes. More importantly, however, they quickly recover from them and tackle the next challenge with optimism. They project an attitude of, "Don't worry about it—I've got the next one."

In basketball coach Bob Knight's book, *Knight, My Story*, he presents an incredible letter he received from legendary coach Claire Bee after the NCAA tournament loss in 1975. (IU was undefeated through the regular season and lost to the University of Kentucky during the tournament.) Here is a piece of that letter, "The young man, the leader, rebounds swiftly from adversity. He has been strengthened by the very blow that cut him down. Now he knows the rough spots that pit the roads and quicksand that lies so innocently nearby. He knows because he has fought his way up that path of agony—almost to the very top. Then suddenly, refreshed by the driving desire that has always inspired young leaders to rush forward and upward, he grasps the new challenge with eager hands and races for the starting line. He will be back."

Trust

No customer can be sustained without trust. No employee can have a lasting relationship with a supervisor without it. No player can build a committed relationship with a coach without trust.

Trust is anchored with people knowing that you will do what

you say you will. It is simple.

Say what you mean; do what you say. Individuals perform best when they trust their leadership. They hold back less of themselves when they know their leadership is authentic. They don't have to particularly like the leadership, but they must trust it to give their very best effort.

When I originally began working on this book, it was under a pretence that Ken Hitchcock and I would be coauthors. I felt the idea of a proven business executive and a proven professional coach collaborating on team building efforts would make for a compelling book. Hitch and I share so many perspectives on team building that it seemed natural. However, I was not prepared to work on the book while leading the sales organization at Texas Instruments. I did not want my team to be confused about who I was and what I thought was important. Was I the chief sales officer or an author? Was I committed to their success and the company's performance or to publishing a book? Hence, I did not start this effort in earnest until I had left Texas Instruments.

Likewise, that is precisely why my friend Hitch did not end up as an author. Although I convinced him to do the foreword and I have often invoked his perspectives, he did not want to send mixed messages to his team, to his ownership, or to the fans. His uncompromising commitment is to the success of the his hockey team, not to promote himself as an author.

With this kind of thinking, I am convinced that we both established foundations of greater trust within our organizations. They viewed our commitment as authentic and completely connected to the same objectives they have. The mutual trust we built allowed us to take the team to the very top. Without trust, optimal performance simply will not be attained.

Trust is also essential when it comes to winning business. When customers trust you, you will be more successful! It is that simple. Customers need a competitive solution, they want to be important to you, and they must trust you!

At Texas Instruments, I often spoke passionately on how customers evaluate an offering along three fundamental characteristics: (1) the solution's performance capability, (2) the total cost of the solution, and (3) the time value of the solution (When can they get it?). Customers have to believe the data you give them as they answer these questions. You cannot break their trust. To do so communicates that they are not really important to you and it will cost you business.

In addition to answering the questions of performance, cost, and time, every customer engagement will need to have credibility along three primary fronts. The customer will have to believe the solution is credible. It will do what you claim it will. Your company will have to be credible. And every person they have engaged with will be evaluated for credibility. Basically, the customer has to "trust" the solution, the company backing the solution, and you!

Maintaining trust is the single most important element of having a high integrity environment, and it is anchored in saying what you mean and doing what you say.

Special Treatment

The fact is, certain performers/players get special treatment. I have heard this declared as an issue of failed integrity, yet I disagree. In most respects, the special treatment is a reflection of value. It is based upon the merits of an individual's achievements. Certain performers are more highly compensated. Likewise, "management" can be more flexible and accommodating in certain situations as well. The key is to keep it clearly linked to performance/contribution. Further, you cannot be flexible on certain requirements you've declared to be of great importance to your team (e.g. making a meeting, work times, treatment of teammates). If you've "laid down the law" on certain topics, you have to hold everyone accountable to the same standard.

Most importantly, the leaders must step in when the "special treatment" impacts the team. I can't provide you with any other hard and fast rules. You will have to be flexible toward the dynamics of your team. The only other alternative is to treat everyone exactly the same; and while that sounds great, it is weak practice. You should not build your rules and processes around your team's lowest common denominator.

Fundamentally, this includes differentiating the rewards you grant. You need to be committed to giving the best rewards to the team members making the biggest contributions. At its core, this is simply capitalism.

Characteristics Of High Integrity Teams

At Texas Instruments we often stressed that organizations with high integrity leadership display the following characteristics.

1. Individuals expect as much of themselves as they do others.
2. Individuals take responsibility for outcomes.
3. Individuals focus on what is right versus who is right.

Adherence To Rules And Standards

It all seems to come back to that issue of conformance to a standard of values. As a leader, you have to articulate what the rules and values are. Then, of utmost importance, you must hold yourself and your team accountable to meeting those rules.

Simplicity in this area will serve you well. Leaders who try to establish too many rules risk diminishing their effectiveness. The key is to establish what is really important and then focus relentlessly upon those areas.

Selecting For Integrity

If there were a single criteria I could select for success, it would be integrity. You can make your resources/team more intelligent through clear role articulation, consistent performance feedback, and a focus on continuous improvement. You can craft a team that consistently demonstrates initiative by rewarding timely action, by reinforcing results, and by establishing a culture where corrected mistakes are acknowledged as inevitable. Integrity, however, really gets to the core of an individual's psyche.

Do your homework. Learn about your resources. Investigate past behavior with a special focus on issues of integrity. Include integrity as an essential element when making decisions about who you want as a part of your team.

You must remember, issues of integrity have disproportionate impact on the individual, the company/team, and the brand.

SUMMARY: THE THREE BEST WAYS
TO ENSURE TEAM INTEGRITY

1. Set the example.
2. Specifically express high expectations for uncompromising integrity.
3. Deal with violations quickly and in an uncompromising fashion.

PUTTING THE PIECES TOGETHER

Role + Sacrifice + Fun = Win

At the risk of unnecessarily extolling the greatness of Ken Hitchcock, I am again compelled to share a great quote he provided me years ago. "Role + Sacrifice + Fun = Win" was the second Hitch "quote" that quickly went up on my whiteboard and stayed there for years. It is a great equation for solving team-building challenges. For years, Hitch has expressed this as one of his favorite equations for success.

First, do the players on your team know their role? This gets us right back to one of the essential elements of making your team more intelligent.

Next, is the team prepared to sacrifice for one another? Can the players accept their role for the good of the team and the outcomes you will achieve? Can individuals defer personal gratification for team success? Do they work hard?

Finally, does the team have fun? Do players bring positive energy to the organization? Do they enjoy the journey?

Enjoy The Journey

In business, in sports, and in life, you are going to face many organizations/teams with great talent. You will even face a lot that are successful. To win consistently, you must build a culture that embraces and enjoys the journey. Yes, the outcome is of paramount importance. Most top leaders will certainly be measured against their ability to achieve great outcomes. Nonetheless, your team will have to enjoy the journey, not just the outcome, if you expect them to win consistently. Said another way, "You better like what you become on your way to the destination."

Your team is much more likely to enjoy their journey if you focus on building intelligence, initiative, and integrity.

Success is likely to come in small steps. You cannot get ahead of yourself when it comes to winning. If you focus on too much success, too much credibility too early, and you are not willing to work and be relentless on a daily basis, then you will not excel in your role. Lose site of your short-term objectives and you will never achieve your long-term goal.

To quote our pal Zig Ziglar again, "You gotta be before you can do, and you gotta do before you can have." Remember that "doing" part normally comes in small steps.

The great news is that time is on your side. Yes, you will have to work hard. Yes, you will have to be relentless. Yes, you will have to embrace initiative. Yes, you should start right now! Yet, as Abe Lincoln said, "The best thing about the future is that it comes one day at a time."

Hard Work

I must return to my favorite quote from Hitch, "Hard work will beat talent if talent doesn't work hard." And while Hitch has never claimed to be the originator of the quote, he has invoked it enough to prove he likes it as well.

To make this necessary "work" most effective, it must have some characteristics.

First, it needs to be intelligent work. That is, the work should be conducted in a manner that is consistent with a specific role. Further, it should be work that is constantly striving to show improvement.

Next, the work must reflect initiative. This work must be conducted with great speed and must be backed by rewards that focus on the result.

Finally, it must be work of high integrity, work that is consistent with the rules and standards established by the organization.

Returning To Roles

Ken Hitchcock has a great tool that he has used to communicate some elements of "role." Here are characteristics that a coach must demonstrate, and then what the coach must instill within the team. You will easily see how this view can be applicable to any business leader as well.

Head Coach:

- Vision: A long-term plan
- Purpose: System, Discipline—Firm Direction
- Trust: Show Strong Character—Candid—Openness
- Action: Strong meaning—Determination—Conviction

Let's dissect those just a bit with intelligence, initiative, and integrity perspective applied.

Vision: A Long-Term Plan

The greater your level of responsibility in an organization, the longer term your vision needs to be. Coaches worry about the team performance over a series of games. They work hard to "stay in the now." General managers think about the season as a whole, about the length of contracts, etc. Engaged owners are likely to focus out as far as the time required to build a dynasty.

The CEO is thinking about creating the future for the company over the next few years. Division heads, heads of sales, etc., are likely to have a disproportionate focus on the next year of performance. The engineer designing the solution is thinking about the key tasks this week. The account manager is focusing on the customer's needs right now.

Having a vision of what must be done is certainly an element of intelligence.

Purpose: System, Discipline—Firm Direction

This is all about both initiative and integrity. Everything about this simple characteristic implies taking action and having accountability.

"When you take the train off the tracks, it is free, but it can't really go anywhere."

In the world of advanced mathematics there is a concept generally referred to as "vector math." It teaches you that vectors have both a magnitude and a direction. You can think of it as a force that can't simply be described by the power behind it, but requires an awareness of direction as well to fully understand it. While an entire team/organization brings the magnitude, the leaders must possess the intelligence, initiative, and integrity to give it a direction.

Or as the Mad Hatter reminds us in *Alice Through the Looking*

Glass, "If you don't know where you are going, any direction will do."

Trust: Show strong character—Candid—Openness

Frankly, this is just another way to describe integrity.

Action: Strong meaning—Determination—Conviction

This is all under the umbrella of initiative. Taking action, getting things done, demonstrating relentlessness are all essential elements of initiative. Additionally, integrity comes into play as well.

Team:

This was Ken Hitchcock's view on what the coach must instill within the team:

- Value: Everyone—no exception—being a piece of something bigger
- Open Communication
- Responsibility: Organization—Team—Family
- Commitment: Each other—System—Willing and eager to sacrifice

Again, we will apply the "Is" to add some color.

Value: Everyone—no exception—being a piece of something bigger

Here the coach is asking the players to show intelligence in terms of understanding what must be accomplished. And he is asking them to show integrity through complete inclusion and the acknowledgement of being a part of something bigger than themselves and their individual accomplishments.

Open Communication

This is a call to say what you mean, a key element of integrity.

Responsibility: Organization—Team—Family

This is a clear call for the standards of value that the organization has established and as such is a direct link to integrity.

Commitment: Each other—System—Willing and eager to sacrifice

If there is a single point in this material that invokes the old "There's no I in team" declaration that we started with, this would be it. Here the coach is clearly expressing a key value of the team. The requirement to commit to the system and to sacrifice for the team are clearly being established as important values. This is part of making the team more intelligent, by communicating expectations, and in establishing a requirement for operating with high integrity.

Generating "Inner Cockiness"

Successful organizations and teams develop an inner cockiness. This is the gut feeling that is generated when teams know that by performing to their capability they will beat anyone. It is not arrogance! Arrogance looks down at the competition. Arrogant teams think of the competition as lower quality or below them. They believe they are better almost by birthright. Arrogant teams don't put in the work required to be consistently successful. Arrogant teams get surprised and get beaten.

I have often heard it said, "Arrogance and conceit are weird diseases. They make everyone sick except the one who's got them."

It might seem strange for me to embrace an "inner" cockiness. Maybe you view it as inconsistent with high integrity. Understand that, while embracing it, I also demand that it be kept inside the team. And

I like it because I know it is born from a healthy kind of confidence. Confidence that is grounded in preparation and hard work. Confidence that is earned. This powerful confidence is hardened by intelligence, initiative, and integrity. The organization believes in itself because it knows there is commitment to the team. Together, the team has learned to give up individual goals for organizational goals. They have proven they will sacrifice for one another, and they have it down to a process.

The most powerful process I can offer you is a relentless focus within your team on intelligence (role—feedback—improvement), initiative (action—results—corrected mistakes), and integrity (example—specific expectation—quickly address violations). Make this a sustainable commitment on your part and it will allow you to build a powerful, winning culture. A culture that breeds a well-earned inner cockiness.

SUMMARY

So now I ask, Are you ready to change the world? Are you committed to leaving a lasting mark within your chosen field? Are you simply looking for a little extra boost in your performance, just enough to secure the slightest of advantages? The answers lie within you. We each get to decide the level of commitment we will bring to the challenges we face. My reminder is that you will accomplish more, get it done more quickly, and have more fun doing it with a strong team. And teams that focus on intelligence, initiative, and integrity will be advantaged.

Developing great teams is important, honorable, and rewarding. You should be proud of what you do. You must commit yourself to perform to the best of your ability in your role.

Every team can be made more intelligent. Every team can build a culture that rewards initiative. Every team can operate with uncompromising integrity. And every team that reflects these characteristics will be better!

Maybe the best news is that "The future dictates the present!" It is your future as a better team builder, team leader, or team member that has you grinding through precisely this kind of material. The more positive outcomes that await you as you embrace and apply these principles are dictating that you focus on ways to improve team performance today.

Even if you only learned a little from this book, you could be on your way to making a major difference for your company, your team, and yourself. In the hyper-competitive world of business and sports the smallest of advantages can make a huge difference.

"Sometimes the difference between ordinary and extraordinary is that little extra."

By building teams with intelligence, initiative, and integrity at the foundation, you've put the right "I" in team, and you have assured your success.

Enjoy the journey!

APPENDIX A

Why a foreword by legendary coach Ken Hitchcock?

As 1999 dawned, I found myself facing my first full year as the head of worldwide sales for Texas Instrument's (TI) semiconductor group. As a company, we had just been through a period of massive reshaping. TI had divested itself of many non-core businesses, including a multi-billion-dollar defense electronics company, a computer company, a contract manufacturing operation, and even the memory business inside our semiconductor group. Our future was clearly in semiconductors, but most specifically in the areas that supported real time signal processing. The divestures were balanced with a set of significant acquisitions, all aligned with our new direction.

Our performance was viewed quite favorably in the financial community. Over a five-year period our stock had gone from about five dollars per share to over twenty-five dollars. In the near future, powered by the "dot-com" boom, TI would be one of many high technology stocks to soar even higher.

The disproportionate focus on signal processing solutions had been paying off in market share gains as well. Not only was the market growing, but we were gaining share. Our profit-sharing program was paying off at a record pace.

I would soon move into a new home in the heart of Dallas and enroll my oldest son in an exceptional school that my wife and I had chosen. Life was good.

Yet, I could not shake a feeling of discomfort from my psyche. I knew something wasn't right. I could feel the momentum slipping away. I did not have the numeric analysis to back up my concerns, but my every instinct told me we were headed in the wrong direction. The obvious market share loss would not reveal itself until the 2000-2001 timeframe. Was something really wrong or did I simply lack the confidence needed to excel in my new role?

My single biggest discomfort was anchored with a concern about over-confidence within my own sales organization. We were starting to get a bit too proud of our results. I had too many people trying to convince customers they should engage with us because we were the clear world leader in our market space. I was concerned that we would not sustain the level of effort required to succeed moving ahead. Our success was making us a big target. Yet, I sensed that our team might not be prepared to continue forward with the kind of commitment that had gotten them to this level to begin with. I personally feared that we were becoming complacent at best and at times even arrogant.

As I searched for a way to address this issue, a voice that kept resonating in my head was that of Ken Hitchcock, head coach for the Dallas Stars at that time. The Stars were just coming off the season in which they had won the Stanley Cup. I am a passionate hockey fan, and I followed the team closely. The championship season had been extraordinary. It was clear that they would be competing with the very best in the 1999-2000 season as well.

Every time I heard Coach Hitchcock speak in detail about the challenges they faced, it seemed that he had a message for me. I found myself going out of my way to listen to his weekly show on the local sports talk radio station. I was fascinated by his relentlessness, his demands for accountability and effort. I also knew instinctively that the challenging of repeating would be even more difficult than winning last year's Cup. Here was a leader who energized me. I had to find a way to engage with him on the topic of establishing and sustaining excellence.

To make a long story short, I reached out and Hitch was there for me. What started as a formal dialog that I would share with my organization (and later, broader groups inside of TI) turned into a genuine friendship. I found that we shared many perspectives. Over time, Hitch became one of my most trusted consults. He helped me on countless occasions. Eventually, he even learned that I could be of some value to him.

As our friendship grew, I found myself extolling the greatness of Hitch's perspectives on many occasions. I also began to document in a better way my own views, tools, and processes. It was this journey that motivated me to share these perspectives and the tools I have used to enable my team's success within a book.

Hitch was the only person I seriously considered asking me to contribute a foreword for this book. As the only hockey coach to ever win a Stanley Cup, an Olympic Gold, a World Cup Championship, and a Junior World Championship, he is a respected and admired friend whom I invoked often throughout the book.

Both of us have a passion for winning—whether championships or market share—and we know that nobody gets there alone. But we also know that a team is made up of people, and each individual's responsibility within a team must never be diminished. Like all effective leaders, we thrive on helping our "players" make the most of their talents as they work together to magnify and multiply those skills. Self-fulfillment and self-sacrifice go hand in hand.

I believe in the metaphoric link between sports and business. Of course, I am a bit of a sports "junkie" as well. I love participating in and observing team behavior and development. The immediacy of the result in the world of sports is addictive. Over the course of the competition you get tangible feedback about the team's performance. The drama is compelling. The battle of wills takes us back to a time when there was much more at stake than a national championship, endorsement contracts, and ESPN Sports Center highlights. Particularly at the elite levels, there will be sacrifice, determination, persistence, and incredible energy expended to secure the victory. Yet, the fortune of empires does not hang in the balance. While it is easy to lose yourself in the adrenaline and hyperbole, it is, however, much safer than the kind of conflicts that play themselves out on the battlefield. Nonetheless, the importance—especially to the participants—should not be underestimated.

Sporting competitions provide the most often invoked metaphor for the world of business. Teams are the reason that these analogies are so often utilized. Business and sports are anchored with a requirement for great team performance. Whether the battle takes place on a sheet of ice, a field of grass, a corporate boardroom, or the retail space in a mall, there will be teams engaged in the battle. It is natural for these metaphors to be used so often. They are relevant to one another. In particular, business organizations respond to the sports-oriented metaphors. In short, they work.

The most striking difference, however, may be the timelines

of business and sports success. Sporting teams have very defined seasons with very specific end-states associated with them. Further, the battles are very distinct (a game-by-game basis) and provide an excellent short-term feedback mechanism. Although owners, general managers, and coaches alike enjoy the prospects of building a dynasty, the business of sports demands a focus, quite distinctly, on each season. In the commercial world, the timelines are most often quite a bit longer. Although the financial community is often disproportionately focused on the quarterly results, most business leaders are disciplined enough to bring a very long-term focus to their efforts. Further, winning key pieces of business and gaining defendable market share is often a multi-year process.

But even with these obvious differences, I have found that I can apply principles we are utilizing in one field and apply them to the other.

With that in mind, I am pleased to have a foreword by Ken Hitchcock.

APPENDIX B

Shaping Perspectives, Author's Background

It is hard for me to read material or listen to a speaker without knowing something about the person's experience to put their views in the proper context. For me, the credibility of the perspective is impacted by what I know about the individual's experiences and accomplishments. Therefore, I find myself compelled to provide some further insight into my background.

I spent the vast majority of my professional career at Texas Instruments (TI). I am lucky to have done so. It is an incredible company, with a rich history in the world of electronics and a legacy of talented, hardworking, and ethical business leaders. I have no doubt that a major portion of my personal credibility comes from my long tenure as a leader at TI. I spent the ten years as a senior sales and marketing leader. I love engaging with customers and facing the challenge of earning business by uncovering a way to deliver superior value. Plus, the sales force at TI is an emotional and fraternal group that gives its leadership a lot of positive energy. It is a fun organization to lead. Additionally, however, my perspectives are impacted by having spent a significant time in general management roles. I have successfully led large P&L centers and done significant product design and development work. I bring a strong general management perspective to every challenge I face.

For many people, TI may still be viewed as "the calculator company." The fact is, TI makes a fine and respected calculator. Yet, that is a very small part of the company (well under ten percent). Take apart any cell phone, DSL or cable modem, HDTV, MP-3 music player, vehicle navigation system, digital video recorder, MRI scanner, notebook computer, network router, or host of other electronic systems, and you are likely to find significant TI content. TI solutions sit at the heart of today's wireless, broadband, and digital consumer electronics world. As the world leader in real time signal processing, TI is enabling the kind of performance that users really want. Those "computer chips" inside really are the heart of modern electronics. While a bit trite, it is true that the semiconductor industry is changing the way people live, work, and play. For an electrical engineer, it is an incredible industry to be a part of, and TI provided an extraordinary culture to learn and grow within.

The proprietary world of advanced analog and digital signal processing technology is significantly different from the one TI operated in as recently as the mid-1990s. In the preface, I mentioned the incredible transformation that changed TI from a diverse electronics conglomerate to primarily a semiconductor company. In the late 1980s, TI's defense electronics business (missiles, radars, etc.) was as large as the semiconductor business. Since that time, TI has divested itself of the defense systems business, a computer products business (they invented the portable computer), a contract manufacturing business, a commodity DRAM business, and more. They also grew the retained portions of the semiconductor business by sixfold. The company was virtually recreated.

A disciplined, focused, hardworking, and insightful leadership team pulled this off. Most of the time, current board chairman Tom Engibous was leading the way. Tom said more with fewer words than anyone I have ever been around. He was relentless in his pursuit of the top objective. If you faced an enormously complex challenge, I placed Tom's ability to find and articulate the single most important issue before you above anyone I had ever met. It was his energy and commitment that brought a determined pace to those major changes. He consistently demonstrated a respect for the importance of initiative with his leadership style.

When I joined the senior leadership team in 1998, I reported to the current CEO, Rich Templeton. Rich was simply the most impressive executive I had ever been around. He was smart, determined, thoughtful, demanding, and driven. I grew up in TI believing Rich was actually my peer. It took me about thirty days of reporting directly to Rich to realize I was not this man's peer. I believe Rich Templeton spent more time thinking about how our customers could be successful than many of their own top executives did. He valued TI's capabilities almost exclusively in the context of what value they could bring the customer base. There may well have been a time when Rich's energy and competitive spirit might have gotten in the way of optimal leadership. However, he demonstrated continuous improvement in every element of his performance. He possessed the intelligence, the energy, and the commitment to provide superior leadership for the next decade, and beyond.

However, even with such extraordinary leadership and a dramatically improved strategic focus, TI's success in the market was not assured. There was early lift with the restructuring, but by about

2000, we were losing market share in the product areas that we had publicly declared as most important to our success. In the strongest upturn of the semiconductor industry, TI lost market share in analog and the digital signal processing market. In the sharpest downturn that closely followed this explosive growth, TI lost market share. Customers were consciously and systematically embracing non-TI solutions in the spaces to which we were most committed.

There were many issues that needed to be addressed within our company. By mid-2000, Rich had structured a more cohesive and effective leadership team. Maybe it was simply time for change, but the new team got better results. Collectively, we communicated more effectively and, therefore, made ourselves more intelligent. We articulated roles more clearly, empowered organizations, and rewarded action, therefore better exploiting an initiative-based culture. And because there was more trust, we operated on a higher plane of integrity that reinforced authenticity, candor, and cooperation. I had seen these principles at work many times in the past and found ways to reinforce them as a means to improve my organization's performance. Watching them work at such a high level gave me the confidence to push forward with this book.

Professional history and performance aside, I want to start earlier in my formative years. The great thing about being a kid is that you really don't know what you don't know. I grew up in Indianapolis in a lower middleclass family. We did not have a lot of extras, but we had what we needed.

What was most relevant about my mother was that she respected education. She reinforced everything about being a good student. My mom grew up on a farm in Northern Indiana, was a very good student, and put herself through nursing school. After marriage, however, she quickly became a stay-at-home mom and concentrated on the family. I think her time in post-high school studies and short stint in the medical field gave her a better appreciation for academic excellence. Once I showed a little academic promise, she encouraged me to reach for more. While neither of my older sisters immediately pursued college after high school, there seemed to be no question that I would follow a collegiate path. My mom set a lot of my value for continuous improvement and intelligence in motion.

My father led a very colorful life, especially in his formative years. I'll save the engaging details for a fictional novel, but it is important to note that he was raised in a boarding house by his fraternal uncle. Like my mom, he was a child of the Depression years. I am confident that growing up in such a period influenced both of them. My mom, however, grew up on a farm; and while she was conscious of the national challenges, her family grew their own food and was minimally impacted. My dad, on the other hand, was a big-city kid all the way. He lived right in the midst of the groups most impacted by the Depression. He saw the powerful impact of extensive unemployment, the loss of homes, and of families torn apart. And growing up around the men in the boarding house meant he garnered his most useful education on the street.

My dad was not much for book smarts. He did not even graduate from high school. As a result, once he gave up his colorful career in the world of gambling, he was ill prepared for much beyond manual-labor anchored jobs. More importantly, however, my dad knew about hard work. He was a traditionalist and wanted his wife to stay at home. As a result, he had to work at least two jobs to provide a marginal standard of living. I learned about hard work from my father. I never remember him having less than two jobs, and often he was working three (one fulltime job, two parttime jobs), at least until my college days. I have no recollection of ever needing shoes;

yet I remember seeing my dad put cardboard in the bottom of his as the soles wore away. What my dad lacked in value for academic preparation he made up for in a commitment to hard work. He truly valued initiative, believing what you were going to do mattered a lot more than how you felt about something.

I took my first paying job when I was ten years old. I sold newspapers out of a stand in downtown Indianapolis. I would ride the bus downtown with my dad on Saturday morning. While he worked his parttime job as a bartender, I sold papers just around the corner from the tavern. I learned early the value of having my own money. My parents did not really encourage saving, but they certainly gave me complete independence over my earnings. Most of it was spent on comics and candy, and I definitely learned to enjoy the fruits of my labor. This was an early lesson on the availability of work, provided you took initiative.

One of the earliest adults I remember impacting my perspective on life was a Kroger store manager by the name of Jim Smith. The summer before I turned sixteen I spent a lot of hours painting houses with my brother-in-law. He worked at Kroger, and each of the houses was owned and kept as rental property by a store manager he knew. That manager, Jim Smith, took a liking to me and my work ethic. He told me to come see him when I turned sixteen and "see about a job." True to his word, Mr. Smith hired he shortly thereafter. It was an incredible job. Bagging groceries may not seem like much, but it paid well. ($2.64 per hour in 1973 was great pay for a sixteen-year-old kid.) It offered great exposure to the importance of customer service and gave me opportunities for professional growth that I remember to this day.

While I started simply bagging groceries, Jim Smith and the Kroger team rewarded my efforts with a chance to learn more important roles and to work more hours. Jim saw that I learned the ropes as a cashier, a produce and dairy department worker, and occasionally on the stocking crew. (They worked the graveyard shift.)

I will never forget the lesson Jim taught me one night when he found me throwing bags with rotten potatoes into the dumpster. Earlier in the day, the head of the produce department had assigned me the task of pulling some bags with bad potatoes off the shelves and disposing of them. It was a simple and clear task; however, one that was full of "missed opportunities," as Jim Smith explained. It was clear that he was disappointed that I so quickly accepted the assignment without seeing any alternatives. More importantly, he worked through his shock and enthusiastically showed an improved outcome. He had me retrieve all the bags I had shucked into the dumpster (there were quite a few). We took them over to a big metal sink. There, we washed the potatoes, carefully removing and disposing of the ones that really had gone bad. The newly cleaned potatoes were then put in a new produce bag and marked for sale at a reduced price. Jim explained how I had just created a great alternative for the less well-off customers at our store and at the same time created a profit stream for our store as well. The cost of my time to clean and re-bag the potatoes was much less than what they would sell for. Our customers would win and so would Kroger.

Jim furthered the lesson by walking around the store and showing me any number of places where this thinking could be applied. I was sixteen years old, and this guy was going out of his way to show me how to be more successful.

During my senior year in high school, Jim decided that I was prepared to run the dairy department while the department head took a two-week vacation over the end-of-the-year holiday period. He let me work exclusively in that area for weeks before and challenged the department head to teach me the nuances required to successfully run the operation. To me it was a big deal. He was rewarding my efforts and commitment in a very public fashion. And the thing that really stands out is how he paid me. For that two-week period, he ensured that Krogers paid me like a dairy department head, which meant about five dollars an hour more than my normal pay!

The summer before my freshman year in college he repeated this opportunity. When the dairy department head left for training as a new store manager, Jim simply said he'd like to use me in that role throughout the summer. That made a big difference in money I could accumulate for school.

My decision to pursue an engineering degree at Rose-Hulman had a significant impact on my development. It was the perfect environment for allowing me to blossom as an adult. Rose-Hulman is an incredible institution. Its current ranking as *News and World Reports* top undergraduate engineering program for eight consecutive years is a testament to what exists at this pristine campus in Terre Haute, Indiana. It is also overly simplistic to associate the school with unmatched academic excellence. Its nurturing culture and commitment to each individual created an environment that allowed me to stretch and grow. I got the kind of attention from faculty and administration that I think parents dream of for their children. It nurtured my mind and stretched my leadership capacity. I think in a bigger institution I would simply have blended in with any number of strong students. At Rose, I gained the confidence and experience to excel as a leader and got attention from faculty and staff that cannot be replicated in larger institutions.

If you want to step out and lead at Rose-Hulman, you have unmatched opportunities to do so. The exposure to the faculty and senior administrative leadership on campus is extraordinary. Your perspectives and expectations are shaped by the time you spend with these leaders. Everyone gets this experience. Certainly, not everyone cultivates their interaction with the same enthusiasm, but I cannot imagine someone graduating from Rose without having been positively impacted by the personal character of the school and its academic and administrative leaders.

There is a long list of great folks at this school who impacted my perspectives. The single greatest impact, however, came from the school's vice president of development and external affairs Ron Reeves. I was lucky to join a fraternity that had Ron as the chapter advisor. Though I saw Ron reach out to numerous students at Rose, it is probably true that his ATO fraternal brothers captured a special place in his heart. We were more than lucky to have such a commanding presence and committed leader as our chapter advisor.

When during my sophomore year it was necessary for me to take on a work-study assignment, Ron reached out and brought me in as part of his team. He led by example in all that he did. His commitment to the students at Rose was matched only by his commitment to the institution itself. He made time for everyone. There was no topic that he was unprepared to engage upon. He was relentless in his pursuit of excellence for the school for all the students he touched. He was my surrogate father on campus and a great mentor, always stretching me to achieve more and showing complete confidence in my capabilities. He operated from a base of unmatched integrity. If I have ever engaged with an individual who reflected true authenticity and a complete commitment to stewardship and honor, it was Ron Reeves. His consistent demonstration of doing the right thing, the right way, has stuck with me for decades.

Ron's integrity level meant that, when he reached out to request a favor, there was a long line of folks ready to lend a hand. The power of his reach was never more impressive than when I was graduating and moving to Texas. I was newly married, just starting my first job, had absolutely no ready cash, and a pile of college debts. Ron asked a Rose alum with connection in the banking industry to help me with an unsecured loan so my wife and I could get off to a smoother start in Dallas. That was all it took. If Ron Reeves endorsed you, you were golden. The only question the bank asked was if I would be interested in opening a checking account with them (which I needed to have anyway). We had the funds to furnish an apartment, buy groceries, and make utility service deposits because Ron Reeves said we were good for the loan. Maybe he cosigned behind the scenes. I don't really know. I just know if you needed help, Ron was there. And if Ron Reeves gave you an endorsement, you were gong to be accepted. The power of authenticity carries a ton of weight. My ongoing support for Rose-Hulman is, in part, an effort to honor Ron Reeves.

Meanwhile, I would love to dazzle you with stories of my athletic prowess. That, however, would require a fictional piece of work. Yes, I loved sports. Yes, I played them growing up, a lot in fact. And no, I was not particularly gifted.

Basketball was my first love. However, being able to play in junior high is a lot different from being talented enough to play in high school. Add a limited skill set to a tiny stature (five foot when I tried out for the freshman basketball team) and you get a young man destined for intramural basketball!

So I concentrated on baseball. It was my second love, and on a relative basis I was better. Not great, mind you, but better. Good enough to play all through high school. My varsity coach told me he'd "never had a player work so hard to be mediocre." He was trying to complement my work ethic, of course.

In a softer moment, he was reinforcing that I should play college ball. He had no concerns regarding my ability to play for Rose-Hulman. He made it clear that I could play for any college team in Indiana. When I asked if he felt I could even make the team at Purdue or Notre Dame, he reiterated his belief, suggesting that what I lacked in athletic talent I made up for with a positive attitude and commitment. "Jeff," he said, "there isn't a coach in this state who wouldn't want you as a part of their team. But please, don't try to make a college team in California, Florida, or Texas. They're going to demand a much higher talent level." Hey, he was right. I was destined for coaching anyway.

After my freshman year in college, I helped my old high school coach with a group of players he had in a developmental summer league. The next summer I was helping my next-door neighbor's Little League team when the head coach bailed out and left the team to me. It was extraordinary. We won a lot of games, finished second in the league, and had a great time. I was clearly a better coach than player, and I was hooked on team leadership. I loved the feeling of stretching an individual's performance. I loved the feedback you get when a team member is succeeding. I thrived on the energy that the team created. I enjoyed the responsibility of helping them get better and achieve more than they thought they could. And I could even deal with the pressure from the parents because any negative aspect was swept away by the positive feedback they gave you when their child excelled. I still have the baseball the kids signed and gave to me after our season ended.

Those two summers and my character growth that had been nurtured at Rose-Hulman gave me the confidence to lead. It reinforced that I would likely succeed and enjoy my journey more if I looked for opportunities to lead. I stepped up within the fraternity, in service organizations on campus, and on the intramural athletic fields. (I had abandoned my baseball dreams, but turned into a very competitive fast-pitch softball player on the intramural fields. You got the competitive thrill of baseball without the time commitment required to succeed in collegiate sports.) Even as I began the search for my first post-college position, I did so with an eye to management. I was confident that I would be more successful in situations where my success was dependent more on team performance than my singular contributions.

To over simplify a bit, my mom embedded a value for education and continuous improvement (intelligence). My dad instilled a value for hard work (initiative). Jim Smith and the Kroger experience allowed me to see many opportunities and made it clear that my performance would be rewarded (initiative). Rose-Hulman provided a laboratory to refine my leadership skills, and Ron Reeves demonstrated the importance and impact of unquestioned integrity.

At Texas Instruments, I became a part of an extraordinary high technology culture that was optimized to reward intelligence, initiative, and integrity. I was given every opportunity I could ask for. While constantly in a demanding environment, I could still learn from the mistakes I made. Most importantly, for almost twenty-five years I saw time and time again how superior team performance led to the best results. When we excelled as a team, our company stood out in an industry that was changing the world.

www.ingramcontent.com/pod-product-compliance
Lightning Source LLC
Chambersburg PA
CBHW022042210326
41458CB00080B/6624/J